The Process of Self-Transformation

The Process of Self-Transformation

Exploring Our Higher Potential for Effective Living

VICENTE HAO CHIN, JR.

This publication has been generously supported by The Kern Foundation

QUEST

BOOKS

THEOSOPHICAL PUBLISHING HOUSE
WHEATON, ILLINOIS • CHENNAI, INDIA

Quest Books
Theosophical Publishing House
PO Box 270
Wheaton, IL 60187-0270

www.questbooks.com

Cover image: JKerrigan/Shutterstock.com
Cover design by Mary Ann Smith
Type design and typesetting by Drew Stevens

Library of Congress Cataloging-in-Publication Data

Chin, Vicente Hao, Jr.
    The process of self-transformation: exploring our higher potential for
effective living / Vicente Hao Chin, Jr.
    pages   cm
"Revised Edition"—Preface.
Earlier edition published in 2003 as The process of self-transformation:
mastery of the self and awakening of our higher potentials.
Includes index.
ISBN 978-0-8356-0935-7
1. Self-control. 2. Self-realization. 3. Self-perception. I. Title.
BF632.C526 2015
158.1—dc23   2014040008

            5   4   3   2   1   •   15   16   17   18   19   20

                Printed in the United States of America

Contents

Preface to the Revised Edition

The roots of human problems lie within the mind and personality of human beings. As long as there are internal contradictions and fragmentation within the psyche of individuals, there will be unhappiness in people as well as conflicts and discord among them.

Since ancient times, whether in the East or the West, sages have known that there are pathways toward the resolution of the inner contradictions within the human soul and the flowering of the full human potential and wholeness. These roads have been tried and tested for millennia and have produced some of the noblest human beings in history.

This book is a modern restatement of this age-old wisdom of humanity supplemented with specific tools that will help in accelerating the transformation of individuals. It was initially presented as a three-day workshop called the Self-Transformation Seminar. Because of the perceived effectiveness of its methods and approaches, it spawned a four-day youth camp for people from the ages thirteen to twenty-five called the Golden Link Youth Camp. Then, because of its impact on the young people who participated in the camps, the Golden Link School was established, which has since become an institution that offers tertiary courses and is now called Golden Link College. The principles of self-transformation became part of the core philosophy of the college. The Golden Link educational system now covers five campuses in various parts of the Philippines.

The workshops of self-transformation have further branched out into courses and seminars on parenting, leadership, peace education, development of corporate culture, marital relationships, stress relief, trauma healing, family healing, effective relationships, meditation, and nurturing the spiritual life. They are all rooted in the same principles of self-change.

This self-transformative approach germinated in the fertile soil of the Theosophical Society in the Philippines, a branch of a worldwide organization that fosters human unity, character building, spirituality, and the quests for truth and human perfection. It promotes these non-dogmatically and in a genuine spirit of freedom. Thus, the self-transformation approach contained in this book grew in a rich environment that benefited from the experiences and insights of various spiritual traditions, philosophies, and sciences.

An important element in this approach is that it is integrative in nature. It combines timeless principles and values with the practical demands of human life. It is not simply a palliative to ease the symptomatic pains of living, nor is it an attempt to primarily adapt to the current demands and values of society. The approach is based on the conviction that the happy and fulfilled life must not be in conflict with the deepest values of human beings, including spirituality and transcendence.

The author is grateful to Quest Books for the suggestion to publish a revised edition. Some parts of the book have been expanded, and it has benefited from the very helpful comments of Richard Smoley, to whom the author is grateful.

—Vicente Hao Chin Jr.
May 2015

Preface

This book was originally intended as a manual for facilitators of the Self-Transformation Seminar that my colleagues and I have been conducting for many years in Asia, Australia, Europe, and North and South America. At the request of seminar participants to have reading materials from the seminar, the book is now available to the general reader, and the materials for facilitators have been put into a separate manual.

The Self-Transformation Seminar receives very encouraging feedback from participants in many countries. They are attended by a wide spectrum of people, including executives, professionals, educators, parents, young people, community development workers, government employees, and peace workers. Many feel that not only is it highly relevant to their present life situations, but also it opens up new dimensions in life to which they had never before given serious thought. We often hear the heartwarming feedback, "I should have learned this when I was younger."

Many schools and universities request that the seminar be given to their administrators, faculty, and students. Religious organizations, nongovernment organizations, professional groups, and private companies similarly request the seminar because of its positive effect on the lives of participants.

Although people who have not attended the seminar can learn the principles of the process presented in the seminar by reading this book, we encourage them to discuss the book with groups or facilitators to ensure that they fully understand the various practices suggested here, especially the self-awareness processing, which is crucial to the entire program. Wherever feasible, we recommend that readers participate in the Self-Transformation Seminar.

Interested persons can visit the Self-Transformation Program website at www.selftransformation.net or write to the Self-Transformation Program, Philippine Theosophical Institute, 1 Iba Street, Quezon City, Philippines. Email: philtheos@gmail.com.

The first drafts of this book have received helpful comments and suggestions from Bebot Rodil, Dr. Caren Elin, Les Vincent, Lionel Rodrigues, Vicki Jerome, Letty Lim, Lourdes Esmero, Diana Dunningham Chapotin, and Barbara Coster, to all of whom I am grateful.

—Vicente Hao Chin Jr.
Quezon City

The Life We Face

From the moment we are born to the day we die, life is a constant balancing act between satisfying personal needs and dealing with external constraints. We face two problems in life: the personal and the social.

The Personal Problem

On the personal level, we are all confronted with the problems of unhappiness, fear, worry, societal pressure, physical and emotional pain, sickness, death, and a thousand other matters that threaten the serenity, meaningfulness, and happiness of life. No one is exempt from these threats. We are born into a life of conflict, and the majority of humanity is born to parents who do not know how to handle life's conflicts. Children learn their parents' faulty ways of coping with these conflicts, thus growing up insecure, defensive, and lost in the jungle of life.

Are there time-tested ways of effectively dealing with these problems? There are. From time immemorial, there have been sages who have discovered and transmitted to later generations enduring solutions to the dilemmas of living. These wise beings have come from diverse cultures, races, and historical periods. Their findings are not secret. They have not kept their discoveries to themselves. Yet, unfortunately, these insights are not as well known to the world as they ought to be. Our educational institutions barely give attention to them, which is regrettable, considering how many school years are devoted to learning polynomials, grammatical rules, historical information, social codes, scientific knowledge, and so on, much of which we don't even use when we become adults.

For example, how many schools teach their children how to handle fear? I don't know of a single one that systematically does so. On the contrary, almost all schools use fear as a tool to compel students to follow rules. Instead of freeing children from fear, they contribute to the accumulation of the children's fears. As a result, children grow up carrying psychological baggage that adds to their unhappiness and unwholesome life patterns.

How many schools teach their students how to deal with worry? Again, I don't know of any. Yet worry is the scourge of humanity. Fear and worry are two of the most unwholesome coping mechanisms of humanity that contribute to human misery. They breed insecurity, which in turn breeds aggressiveness, which eventually begets violence.

Yet enough is known about how to handle fear and worry that billions of human beings should be able to live with fewer burdens and less misery. That the educational establishments in all countries have not incorporated such basic insights into their curriculum is a sad commentary on our collective wisdom. Humanity today is more concerned about earning a living than with learning how to live. People are more occupied with how to compete than how to excel. They are too busy building up protective defenses to guard their insecurities and have very little time to explore their higher potentials as human beings.

For many years I have been involved in conducting study groups through the Theosophical Society on such subjects as spirituality, transpersonal consciousness, meditation, karma, and destiny. Initially, I could not help but notice that, although these ideas were eagerly accepted, this knowledge was not becoming integrated into people's daily lives, as was obvious by some people's attitudes and behaviors. For example, speakers and participants would talk about qualifications for the spiritual life, which include the cessation of anger and selfishness, yet there were no sessions devoted to how to actually handle anger and selfishness.

A gap clearly existed between the ideal and the actual. Discussions about the ideal can often lull us into thinking that we are going in that direction, when in fact we are not. We feel satisfied that we are studying it, that we know about it, but strangely, we are not worried that we do not live it.

The Self-Transformation Seminar arose out of this need to bridge the gap between the ideal and the actual. If we talk about love, what exactly do we mean in terms of our relationships with our spouses and children, our friends, coworkers, and others? Is love a verbal declaration? Is it a behavioral expression of care? Or is it a state of consciousness within? Or all of these? How do we actualize each one? What are the obstacles in the way of their realization?

The proof of the pudding is in the eating, we have heard it said. Hence, we must ask questions about the results of our studies and the declarations of our ideals. Is there really inner peace in our daily lives? Are we free of fear and chronic worry?

Are we easily hurt when someone unthoughtfully says something unkind to us? Do we get depressed? Do people around us sense or feel our care for them?

The Self-Transformation Seminar teaches that it is possible for a person to grow toward states of serenity and meaningfulness, with the capacity to effectively deal with the unavoidable conflicts in living. One can be free from the shackles of fear, anger, and resentment and awaken to the possibility of genuine love and caring. The Self-Transformation Seminar affirms that it is possible to explore the higher potentials of human life—such as spirituality, intuition, and transcendence—without having to abandon the circumstantial duties we are born into or grow into.

The Social Problem

The social problem must inevitably be faced by the individual. One cannot escape from it. Even if one goes to the mountains to withdraw from people, such a withdrawal is in itself an attempt to deal with the problems of human relationship, whether they are interpersonal, societal, or global.

Interpersonal

If we ponder on it, we will find that virtually all of our unhappiness is due to problems in relationships. As one friend put it, "I know what hell is. Hell is people." When we read of businesspeople who commit suicide because of business failures or bankruptcy, they do so not because of money but because of the fear of humiliation. Psychologists have observed that the number one fear is that of rejection (which includes fear of failure and fear of public speaking). We fear rejection more than death and pain.

When we look into the conflict, anger, fear, and resentment in interpersonal relationships, we find that they are rooted in our individual conditionings, attitudes, and characters. Fear, for example, is the result of conditionings by our elders, schools, or the media. Thus, to deal with fear, it is not the object of fear that we must look into, but the conditionings that we have acquired. We need, then, to transform ourselves, not other people.

Societal

The social environment is another source of chronic human problems. This includes crimes, tyranny, loss of freedom, injustice, corruption, competition, and other forms of social disorder. Many thinkers have inquired into the nature of the ideal society, ranging from Plato in his *Republic* to Thomas More in his *Utopia*. Two and a half thousand years of such inquiry have not made the world a more ideal place. In many ways, it has become worse.

In the meantime, the legal structure of society has become more and more complex. Every year, thousands of new laws are enacted, from national congresses to the smallest town councils. They complicate life, and we find that we are still very far from the utopia we seek. There is one fundamental reason why we cannot create that ideal society. That reason is us—we human beings. Because of our very own present natures, no ideal society is possible.

More than twenty years ago, I visited Auroville, the visionary community in South India established in honor of Sri

Aurobindo, the famous yogi. A guide took us around. The residents numbered several thousand and came from various countries around the world. Before they were accepted as residents, they had to go through probation, which, I learned, took almost a year. Along with residential houses, Auroville had a school, small factories, and stores. But one place the guide mentioned struck me: it was the *free store*. It was like any other store, except that if you saw anything in the store you wanted, you could have it—for free. The only request made of you was that if you had anything in your house you didn't need, you would donate it to the store. I asked the guide how long the store had been in existence.

"Two and a half years," he said.

"What is the difference between the store now compared to the beginning?" I asked.

"Well, today there are more items in the store than at the beginning."

I thought about Manila, the city where I had come from, and realized that it would not be possible at all to put up such a store there. When I ask audiences in various places what would happen if they put up such a store in their cities, they invariably laugh. "It would last only one day, and everything would be gone." Some even say it would take only one hour.

What is the difference between our cities and Auroville? Why can't we do what is possible in Auroville? The answer is the people. Those who join Auroville, I presume, are individuals who have gone beyond the acquisitive and greedy attitudes of the average citizen of the world. They see that cooperation and mutual concern are the keys to social stability and harmony. It drove home to my mind that indeed, if we want our societies to change, we must start with the individuals who compose such societies. Where there is no individual transformation, society will remain essentially stagnant, despite dazzling technological advances.

More than fifteen years after my visit, I went back to Auroville to see if the free store was still in existence. What do you think I saw? There were now two free stores.

Sometime after my first visit to Auroville, the world witnessed the crumbling of the communist states in Eastern Europe and the Soviet Union. In a very short time, almost all of those states discarded communism and went back to the free enterprise system. Naturally, there was a widespread observation that, after seventy years of experimentation, communism had failed. Marx had been proven wrong.

But amidst all these commentaries about the failure of communism, one thing seems to have gone unnoticed: we forget that communism is successfully thriving all over the world. It has been and continues to be implemented by numerous communities that have lasted for hundreds of years without coercion or threat. The members of such communities are apparently happy staying within such communistic societies, for they are free to leave anytime they want to, without reprisal or condemnation. In fact, they seem to be a happier lot than the rest of us. Who are these groups?

These are the monastic and religious orders in the various religions of the world: the Buddhist monks, the Trappist monks, the Jesuit order, the Carmelites, and so on. These communities implemented the famous dictum of Marx centuries before Marx was born: from each according to his ability, to each according to his needs. The able and healthy members of such communities work earnestly without additional monetary incentives, and the weak and feeble ones receive care even if they hardly contribute to the work of their community. There is little complaint about such inequality, and we don't hear of court cases filed against unfair compensation.

Why couldn't the former Soviet Union, with its vast military and police powers, carry out the communistic principles of Marx, but these religious communities could, without the benefit of even a security guard to impose discipline among themselves?

Again, we are compelled to conclude that the difference is the people. It is not the rules, not the laws, that make the essential difference. It is the people. The citizens of the socialist countries, as much as those of the capitalist countries, are generally self-centered, acquisitive, and covetous individuals who may be willing to violate laws in order to meet their wants and desires. The people in the spiritual communities, on the other hand, have, to a certain extent, transcended the selfish, acquisitive tendencies of the layperson.

In the business world, competitors are ready to wipe out each other. Why? Why can't they agree to live and let live? Again, it is due to mutual insecurity and distrust, two attitudes that are at the root of a host of social problems. While these negative attitudes remain within us, true social harmony will remain an elusive dream.

Global

For about five thousand years of recorded history, war has been the scourge of humanity. Everybody—with very few exceptions—does not like war. No mother would like to send her children to the battlefields. We associate war with barbarism, from a time when human beings were governed by their amygdalas (the mammalian brain) rather than by their frontal lobes. As we have become more civilized, however, we have become more sophisticated and less barbaric, and yet we have become more capable of evil than before. Wars have become more harrowing. Instead of bows and arrows, we use land mines, biological weapons, poison gases, and nuclear bombs, all of which kill not only the so-called enemies, but also innocent civilians, women, and children, who have nothing to do with the political or military agendas of the leaders.

Albert Einstein was once asked what kind of weapon will be used in World War III. He said, "I don't know. But I know what they will use in World War IV. They will use stones."

Do pacts and treaties solve the problems of war? The lessons in the twentieth century are proof that, at best, they are the lulls between storms. The First World War was widely considered as the last war. But barely twenty years later, a worse world war broke out, unleashing the most frightful weapons humanity has known: the V2 bombers and the atomic bomb.

During the Second World War, a total of 56.4 million people died. We assume, that since its end in 1945, the world is now enjoying more than half a century of peace. Right? Wrong In the past half century, according to the Stockholm International Peace Research Institute, more than 20 million people have been killed because of wars and conflicts in various parts of the world.

The solution to global conflicts cannot be found in arms buildups that are meant to serve as deterrents. Neither can it be found in treaties and agreements, though they are very helpful in creating interim peace. The solution can only be found in our collective maturity, when a significant percentage of the world's population have transcended the personal and social conditionings at the root of international insecurity, fear, and distrust, and when they have awakened a higher level of consciousness that sees humanity as an indivisible family, regardless of color, religion, nationality, or race.

The Self-Transformation Process

The self-transformation process is an approach to the inner change necessary for resolving both the personal and the social problems of life. The process is not new. It is found in wisdom traditions all over the world, both ancient and modern. Research continues to affirm the validity of the principles of the self-transformation process.

In 1995, the exercises used in this approach were developed into a seminar called the Self-Transformation Seminar. It has since been given to thousands of people, both young and old, in many countries, including the Philippines, Australia, United Kingdom, Singapore, Malaysia, Indonesia, India, the United States, Brazil, Israel, and others. The participants' responses have been very positive. Some say they desire to not only continue the process, but also learn how to conduct the seminar and become facilitators. Training courses for facilitators have been established in several countries.

The Nature of Self-Transformation

The self-transformation program described in this book is an approach to self-integration, which serves as a foundation for effective living. It also provides an indispensable basis for long-term interpersonal, societal, and global peace, as well as a necessary preparation for the spiritual life.

Self-transformation consists of four aspects: (1) review of one's personal map of reality; (2) clarification of one's values; (3) self-mastery; and (4) transcendence. Each aspect is an essential part of the whole. When one is missing, the transformation process is not fully integrated.[1]

Internal sources of conflict and discordance will continue to be present. The fourth aspect, transcendence, usually comes later in life to most people. But its beginnings can be found when we have clarified our values and developed self-mastery.

Review of Our Personal Map of Reality

We are products of our conditionings, which are specific reaction patterns to given stimuli, such as to sounds, objects, individuals, professions, animals, memories, or situations. In this book, we use the word "conditioning" to refer to the set of behaviors and thought patterns that have been acquired—often uncritically—from experience, including beliefs and attitudes. Thus we use it here in a broader sense than how it is commonly used in psychology (classical and operant conditioning). Cultural attitudes and religious beliefs, for example, would be part of such conditionings, to the extent they have been implanted by society into the mind of the person. How we behave, how we feel, how we think, our attitudes, likes and dislikes, our beliefs and outlooks—all these are the fruits of conditionings. We pick up and acquire these conditionings as we grow up, starting from the womb. They constitute our worldview, our map of reality. Our attitudes and fears, the college courses we choose, the husband or wife we select, our favorite foods, the leisure we prefer—these are but the results of long causal chains that originate from basic conditionings. And they determine the quality and meaning of our lives, our happiness, or our unhappiness. They determine our destiny.

Unfortunately, conditionings are not well designed. We acquire them unsystematically and often unconsciously, resulting in unwholesome reaction patterns, such as fear and prejudice, that make life miserable and ineffective. Such conditionings can border on pure superstitions, and one may be unaware of them.

Edna, a college graduate, worked as a corporate secretary in an export manufacturing company. Her husband also had stable employment. Yet every month she would go around borrowing money or asking the company to advance her salary. I was one of those whom she regularly approached for a loan, and I couldn't help but ask her, "Don't you and your husband have enough savings from your income?" "No, we don't," she replied. "Why?" She explained, "My mother, who lives with us, gets angry when we keep any savings, whether at home or in the bank. She says that when we try to save, we are preparing for some misfortune and will attract such a misfortune. She says it is bad luck." I was really surprised by this answer. So I asked her, "Do you mean to say that your savings will be bad luck to you, but that our savings is good luck to you since you are borrowing from us?" This made her pensive for some moments, and then she looked at me. "I will now start saving money, even if my mother gets angry with me."

Edna and her husband eventually had a second house, a business, and enough money to send all her children to private education. Where did these all come from? Her savings. If she had not rectified her map of reality, she would be borrowing right and left for the rest of her life.

As children, we don't have a choice in these conditionings. Our elders and our environments, such as school, TV, and media, imposed them upon us. We are, in effect, victims of our conditionings. When we don't review them, we continue to be helpless victims throughout our lives.

The transformation process must therefore review all these conditionings, and it must start with our worldview, our understanding of what life is all about. For example, our worldview about the purpose of life is greatly determined by our parents. We grow up exposed to what is significant to our parents—the profit and loss of a business, the problems in the office, the fear of committing sins, the need to go to church every

Sunday, and so on. Day by day, what we see and hear from our parents and elders constitute the bricks and stones that build the edifice from which we look out into the world. When this edifice is constructed with windows that have distorted glass panes, we then see life distorted, and we become ineffective in dealing with it. Our solutions do not work because we cannot understand the problems. Because we cannot deal with the problems of living, we complain that life is cruel, unfair, fearful, or oppressive. Then we behave defensively or withdraw and become timid losers, or toughen ourselves by becoming aggressive or being bullies.

This tangled and convoluted network of conditionings is difficult to see and difficult to undo. The average person walks through life carrying out, almost unconsciously, the patterns of such conditionings—living and behaving according to the grooves etched since infancy.

In a profound sense, we are asleep. We move like robots and automatons, dutifully carrying out the confused programming in our psyches. The first stage to enlightenment is to be aware that we are moving mechanically according to pre-established, conditioned patterns. When the Buddha, the Enlightened One, was asked, "What is the difference between yourself and other people?" he replied, "There is no difference between me and other people except that I am awake."

This continuous review of one's personal map of reality is a never-ending process. But when a person starts the self-transformation process, certain elements of this knowledge are essential to effect change. I touch on these in chapter 3.

Clarification of Values

After one's conceptions about life have been reviewed, then two things must be clarified: the principles upon which one's actions will be based, and priorities. This means the values by which to guide one's life must be clarified. Values are objects or principles that are worth pursuing, or worthwhile. It is worthwhile to have inner peace; hence, inner peace is a value. There are three kinds of values.

Universal or Core Values

These values are embraced by all human beings, either because of the intrinsic nature of the values or because of the very nature of being human. For example, truth as objective reality (as distinguished from truthfulness) is sought for its own sake, because it doesn't make sense to pursue unreality unless one is psychologically unbalanced. The intrinsic nature of truth makes it a universal value. There are also values that are sought universally because of human nature. Happiness, for example, is sought by all human beings because we are psychologically and biologically constructed that way. No one deliberately pursues unhappiness. Even masochists pursue self-satisfaction.

Social and Cultural Values

These values change according to time and place. Reviewing them is extremely important to free oneself from conditionings. Many of these values are unconsciously acquired; they are unquestioned and tend to dominate a person's outlook and thinking. In many ways, people identify so much with the values of their culture that changing their values seems like changing themselves. Changing one's values is a decision that must be faced, for many social, cultural, and religious values are obstacles to wholesome growth, psychologically and spiritually. Some of what are called religious values belong to this category, while some belong to the universal values category.

Personal Values

These values are what is worthwhile to an individual and will differ from person to person. One person may value solitude, and another may appreciate company. One person may give supreme weight to family matters, another to career.

It is important to understand that inner peace and social harmony are not attainable when cultural, social, and personal values are contrary to universal values. Thus, a fundamental principle in self-transformation is that personal values must be brought into alignment with universal values. But to do so, we must understand the validity and worthiness of universal values.

In the chapters that follow, the discussion on values is placed after self-mastery. Although values should logically precede self-mastery, I have learned from experience that people find it difficult to appreciate the integration of universal values into their lives unless they have dealt with conflicts within themselves.

Self-Mastery

If we have an inkling of what is worth pursuing in life, can we actually pursue it? Can we climb the mountain of our dreams and not just dream about it? Or is it too difficult? Are there too many obstacles?

First of all, we need to see that the principal obstacle to pursuing our visions is ourselves. It is not circumstances or other people that make the journey hard. We are our worst enemies. While we have the potential to transform our lives and reach our highest ideals, we often get trapped in the fundamental mistake of blaming outer circumstances for our failures. The failures come from within.

Self-mastery is a crucial key in the self-transformation process. It is the most important step that leads to change. With it, we can gain insights about our own natures and the internal dynamics of our psyches and bodies. At the root of self-mastery are two important ideas: self-awareness and freedom from unwholesome conditioning. The first one is the key to the second. The second one is the key to liberation.

To attain self-mastery, we have to look at certain aspects of the personality, such as:

- Anger

- Fear

- Resentment and hatred

- Automatic reactions

- Moods, depression, loneliness

- Needs

- Self-centeredness

In this discussion of self-mastery, the topic of effectiveness in relationships needs special attention. Aside from dealing with conditionings, it is essential to learn fundamental approaches to effective relationships. Hence, chapter 15 is devoted to this topic.

Transcendence

The pinnacle of self-transformation is the discovery of our higher nature—our true nature. This realization frees us from the prison of the personality or the vehicles we use. As mentioned above, the personality is essentially a product of conditionings, and we are virtually prisoners of such conditionings. The discovery of that which is beyond the personality is the key to freedom. When mystics speak about liberation or *moksha*, of being awake, of being self-realized, they refer to this transcendent freedom. It is a journey worth pursuing, because otherwise we are wallowing in this prison.

The true motivation for self-transformation is inner discontentment, the "divine discontent" of which mystics speak. It is a yearning that does not arise from conditionings, but rather from the flowering of an inner nature that transcends the outer personality. It is divine because it emanates from our spiritual nature rather than our conditioned desires and ambitions. When our motivation is merely to become better, or to improve ourselves, or to be more successful or effective, then the impetus for transformation will be short-lived. It will stop when we cease to feel the pressure of the problems that goaded us to improve ourselves, even if we haven't really improved ourselves.

Transcendence refers to an expanded state of awareness and experience that goes beyond the ordinary levels of doing, feeling, and thinking. It is a realization of our full potential, of what we can become. But it also brings us beyond mere self-mastery to a fuller understanding of the nature of life and the cosmos. Through it, we cease to be prisoners of this world-cage in which we typically find ourselves.

The transcendent consciousness is the true integrating factor within us. When it awakens, we become aware of an inner compass that guides our lives, and we are then able to determine which conditionings are wholesome and which ones are not. This consciousness also becomes aware of conflicts and is the inner judge of how such conflicts should be resolved. Prior to its awakening, the destiny of the personality is determined by external conditioning, and conflicts are resolved by the conditioning (e.g., fear, desire, beliefs, resentment) that is stronger. But when this higher consciousness is awakened, it can diminish the control of these conditionings.

True inner peace is rooted in the awakening of the transcendent within us. This insight is well proven by the independent experiences of sages over thousands of years. But it doesn't mean withdrawal. Transcendence is not a rejection or a rebellion. We simply grow beyond the current limits of our understanding. We continue to appreciate and apply the usefulness of our previous understanding but in the new light of this wider understanding. Just like when we outgrow our childhood toys, we don't reject them. We are free to play or not play with them, but they no longer play a central role in our lives. We see them as they really are, rather than as treasures we must guard with teeth and fists, as we did when we were children, when we weren't willing to let go of them or even lend them to others.

The self-transformation process described in this book covers the four aspects of self-transformation: (1) review of the personal map of reality, (2) clarification of values, (3) self-mastery, and (4) transcendence. To most people, however, the first three have the greatest relevance. This is natural. The fourth stage, transcendence, is something that has to emerge spontaneously. It is not something that can be forced. Working on the first three, however, will nurture and induce the emergence of the fourth.

Spirituality and Self-Transformation

Many people ask if it is necessary to work on physical, emotional, and other psychological factors in order to pursue the spiritual life. Yes, it is. The reasons are straightforward and should be obvious, but for some reason many people who aspire to what they think is the spiritual life often choose to ignore the need to attend to their worldly being. In effect, they choose the way of suppression and denial, which in both the short and long run become obstacles to the transcendent life. Conflicts or weaknesses in the personality draw the consciousness to these levels. We identify with these issues through attachment.

Two kinds of preparation are needed for the spiritual life. The first is purification, the second is structure building. Purification is the cleansing of the unwholesome conditioning in the personality, such as fear, guilt, resentment, and proneness to anger. Structure building is the strengthening of one's capabilities for dealing with the complex circumstances in life. Timidity denotes a weak psychological structure. Assertiveness is a healthy structure. Primacy of will over habits is healthy. Chronic laziness is not; it means that the outer vehicles are not well integrated with one's higher nature.

Spirituality is not disconnected from physical or psychological experiences. The spiritual life is not separate from the worldly life. When there is weakness in one facet, it affects the other.

Self-transformation, therefore, has a dual thrust: the transformation and purification of the outer personality and the awakening and strengthening of the inner self. This dual thrust assumes a third aspect: the harmonious interaction between the higher self and the lower self, making the lower subservient to the higher.

Our Human Nature

In the self-transformation process, we review the following aspects of the reality map:

- The nature of the human being

- The effects of conditioning in human life

- The power to change conditioning and mold our destiny —self-initiative

- Human perfectibility

Other topics such as karma, life after death, rebirth, and the unity of life are also important in such a review but are not discussed in this book.

The Nature of the Human Being

The study of human nature is the key to the self-transformation process. It is the foundation of many insights, principles, methods, and approaches that are taught in the seminar. It is therefore important that we should have an understanding of human nature and be able to verify its validity from our own observation and experience. We should similarly be familiar with the correspondence of our understanding of human nature with the teachings of spiritual traditions around the world.

We have levels of consciousness, as shown in figure 3.1. Human experience, including our reactions to external events, can be better understood when we are familiar with these strata of consciousness.

Physical Body

The physical body is composed of the dense material body—the solid, liquid, and gaseous content of the physical body—and the etheric double, the "bioplasmic body," whose emanations can be recorded by Kirlian photography. It is an exact replica of the dense body but is composed of ethereal material invisible to the normal eye (although a very small minority of people can see these emanations). The glow coming from this body is what has been traditionally called the human aura.

The etheric double is the vehicle for the circulation of what is known as *ch'i* (*qi* in pinyin), or *prana*. This energy is the same as Wilhelm Reich's *orgone* and Baron von Reichenbach's *odylic* or *odic* force. The British physician W. Kilner called the emanations the *human atmosphere* and wrote his researches in a book of the same name (later retitled *The Human Aura*).[1] Dr. Thelma Moss, who has conducted numerous researches on this force through Kirlian photography, calls it bioenergy.[2]

The knowledge of this etheric double and the energy it transmits is very important in understanding certain phenomena that have puzzled humanity for centuries. It is behind

PLANES OF CONSCIOUSNESS	SANSKRIT EQUIVALENT	
Spirit	*Atma*	Individuality or inner self
Transcendent/spiritual	*Buddhi*	
Higher mental	*Arupa manas*	
Lower mental	*Rupa manas*	
Emotional	*Kama*	
Physical • Etheric double • Dense body	*Linga sarira* *Sthula sarira*	Personality or outer self

FIGURE 3.1. **Levels of Human Consciousness**. The levels of human consciousness are divisible into two distinct groups: the individuality and the personality.

what is called magnetic healing, healing by the hand, or *pranic* healing. Mesmerism, popularized by Anton Mesmer, is possible only through the manipulation of this energy. It involves changes in the etheric double and the movements of the vital energy, which Mesmer called *animal magnetism*. Mesmerism is often mistakenly considered as identical with hypnotism, but the latter is only a psychological phenomenon that enables the hypnotist to give direct instructions to the subconscious without the censorship of the conscious ego, while mesmerism is control or manipulation of the vital energy that affects not only the body, but also the mind.

The control over this etheric double and its energy explains such phenomena as suspended animation, in which fakirs are buried for days without food and oxygen and remain alive; telekinesis, or the capacity for the mind to move physical objects; and psychic surgery, in which the physical body is opened with bare hands and closed without scars.

This energy is also behind the documented phenomena of people who remain alive and healthy without taking food and liquid for decades, such as Therese Neumann of Konnersreuth, Germany, and Giri Bala of India.[3] It is the basis of *ch'i kung* (*qigong*) practice and healing, acupuncture, and shiatsu therapy.

Emotional Body

Called *kama* in Eastern traditions, the emotional body is another stratum or plane of consciousness closely connected to the physico-etheric structure. It is the seat of emotions and becomes a separate body after the death of a person.

Lower Mental Level

The lower mental level is the level of concrete thought, such as when we think of specific objects like a particular chair or horse or person or word. Thoughts on this level have either form, color, shape, name, or sound. Hence, in Sanskrit, this mental faculty is often called *rupa manas* or *form-mind*. Theosophical literature refers to it as the *concrete* mind.

Higher Mental Level

Abstract or conceptual thinking occurs on the higher mental level of consciousness. Thoughts here are without form, hence are called *arupa manas* or *formless mind*. For example, when we understand the essence of infinity, we don't think of particular images of objects. To understand infinity, we don't need to imagine black space (although we almost automatically do). If we imagine outer space with stars and planets, it is the concrete mind functioning.

Transcendent Level

At the transcendent level lies the sphere of spiritual, contemplative, or mystical consciousness, called *buddhi* or *prajna* in the East. True intuition occurs in this sphere. Intuition is not the same as extrasensory perception such as telepathy or clairvoyance. The latter group belongs to the personality, whereas intuition belongs to the individuality.

Like the other planes of consciousness, the transcendent plane has many subplanes and aspects. Illumination, or enlightenment, occurs on this plane. Such illumination has multiple levels, called by various kinds of *samadhis* or *satoris* in the East. This subject is touched on again when we discuss transcendence in a later chapter.

Spirit or Higher Self

The experience on the spirit, or higher self, is referred to by St. Teresa of Avila as *union*, as distinguished from illumination. It is the pinnacle of the mystical life. It is the nirvana of Buddhism. One who has attained this state is called a self-realized individual, that is, one who has attained the deepest realization of one's true nature. Theosophists refer to this as the realization of one's *atma* nature.

A Human Being's Dual Nature

The six planes described in the previous section (or seven, if the physical is considered as dual) are divisible into two important groups: the individuality and the personality, or the higher (inner) self and the lower (outer) self. Each group can be symbolized by a triangle, one upright and the other inverted (see figure 3.2). Each group has distinct characteristics, the understanding of which is vital to self-transformation.

The lower triangle, or the personality, is a product of conditioning and behaves primarily in response to that conditioning. It is driven by desires and needs, and thus it is self-centered. The personality thinks in terms of what benefit it can gain from something or what pain it can avoid. The higher triangle, or individuality, is different. The higher mind is objective in viewing things and hence is fair and impersonal.

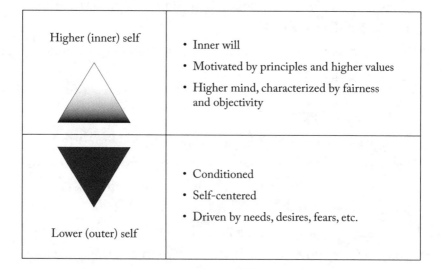

Higher (inner) self	• Inner will • Motivated by principles and higher values • Higher mind, characterized by fairness and objectivity
Lower (outer) self	• Conditioned • Self-centered • Driven by needs, desires, fears, etc.

FIGURE 3.2. The Higher and Lower Selves. The higher (inner) and lower (outer) selves have certain distinct characteristics.

Whom Would You Like to Win?

To understand the difference between the higher mind and the personality, answer this question: if your child were a participant in a contest, whom would you like to win the contest? (Pause a moment to answer the question before reading further.)

Virtually everyone will answer, "my child." Nothing unusual. However, don't you also want the best contestant to win, whether or not that contestant is your child? (Pause a moment to consider this question.)

Most people will say, "Yes, I want the best contestant to win." (A few will be honest enough to admit that they still want their child to win, even if their child is not the best.)

Now try to answer again: if your child were a contestant in a contest, whom would you like to win the contest? (Pause again to consider.)

Many people will answer, "I want the best contestant to win," and many will remain silent.

For those of you who say that "the best contestant should win," don't you also want, at the same time, your child to win?

Almost everyone will nod his or her head in answer to this question. In other words, whatever your answer is, you will almost always have a second answer. This is because you have a dual nature. And the answers from the two natures are often in conflict with one another.

CHAPTER THREE

The Conflict between the
Higher and the Lower Selves

We have here an important insight that is a key to the self-transformation process. We human beings have a dual nature. The two different answers come from these two different natures, the higher and the lower selves. The lower self, or the personality, wants its child to win—for it is basically self-centered and driven by desire. The higher mind, however, is impersonal and hence is more capable of seeing things without being influenced by the colored glasses of desires. It sees immediately the truth that the best contestant should win.

People whose lower selves are dominant tend to work toward having their children win. They may even bribe or blackmail the judges. People whose higher minds are dominant are able to gladly accept their children not winning. They immediately see (or intuit) that it is fair and right that the best contestant should win, even if it is not their own child.

Here is a tremendously significant implication of the above observation about the tendencies of the higher and lower selves: People who are dominated by their lower personalities are candidates for disappointments, frustrations, and unhappiness, and they are also capable of doing injustice to achieve their ends. They are the sources of the trouble spots in this world.

Individuals whose higher selves are dominant, on the other hand, are people who can accept reality as it is. They see more clearly what is right and what is not, and are not unhappy with the consequences when these are based on the right principles. These people tend to be happier, more at peace, and more contented than those whose lower selves are dominant.

Further Readings

Certain books are helpful in the further study of human nature as outlined above. I encourage you to become familiar with the theosophical presentation of the various planes of consciousness and suggest the following books:

The Ancient Wisdom by Annie Besant (Adyar: Theosophical Publishing House).

The Key to Theosophy by H. P. Blavatsky. There are many editions of this work. Some are abridged. The original is published by Theosophy Company (Los Angeles) and the Theosophical University Press (Pasadena).

In the past century, many different classifications about the levels of human consciousness have been made, and an attempt to compare many of them will be found in *Integral Psychology* by Ken Wilber (Boston: Shambhala, 2000). This book has multiple charts that compare the stratification of consciousness by such writers and groups as Aurobindo, Piaget, Sufism, Kabbalah, Vedanta, and Buddhism.

Among theosophical writings, in the past one hundred years some changes have been made in the classification and nomenclature regarding the planes of human consciousness. In the early literature, particularly the writings of H. P. Blavatsky, the four principles of the lower personality consisted of *kama* (emotions), *prana* (vital energy), *linga sarira* (the etheric double), and *sthula sarira* (the physical body). Later literature gives emphasis to the vehicles, or planes, and considers *prana* as an energy that flows through the vehicles.

H. P. Blavatsky also used the term *astral body* to refer to the *linga sarira*. Later writers such as Annie Besant and C. W.

Leadbeater used the term *astral body* to refer to the emotional body, or *kama rupa*. Hence, to avoid any confusion, the term *astral body* has not been used in this book.

The Nature of Human Conditioning

The realization that our personalities are the products of conditioning is extremely important and forms another key to the self-transformation process. The primary conditionings that are most susceptible to internal and external conflicts are the following:

- Fear reactions

- Prejudices, likes, and dislikes

- Resentments and attachments

- Coping mechanisms such as stress, irritation, and anger

The field of behavioristic psychology arose out of the realization of the overwhelming power of conditioning in the life of an individual. B. F. Skinner, the well-known exponent of behaviorism, claimed that he would be able to produce any kind of human being—priest, soldier, criminal, businessperson, and so on—if a person were entrusted to him from babyhood to adulthood.

Although behaviorism is seriously inadequate as a framework for the understanding of the human psyche, it validates the central role of conditioning in the formation of the thinking, attitudes, reaction patterns, and habits of individuals.

Conditionings can go deep into the subconscious, and this is where they do their maximum harm (or benefit). A person may have been frightened by a cat while still young. If this fear was not processed properly by the conscious mind, it would go to the individual's subconscious mind. To that person, all cats may be frightening from that time on.

When we learn to drive, we first have to consciously decide to step on the brake when we see a red light or a person crossing the street. After repeated actions along these lines, we become conditioned to step on the brake when we see a red light. We do this even in the middle of a conversation with somebody else. It is done without deliberation or thought. In fact, it may be said that drivers don't even decide to step on the brake— their conditioning acts automatically.

Push Buttons

Each conditioning is a push button in the subconscious mind. When a specific type of stimulus is perceived, the button of one type of conditioning is pushed, triggering an automatic reaction. A simplified diagram can help illustrate how the push buttons are accumulated (see figure 4.1).

An emotionally distressing experience passes partly through the conscious mind and partly through the peripheral consciousness. The conscious mind can directly feel and process the distress, but the peripheral consciousness tends to reject

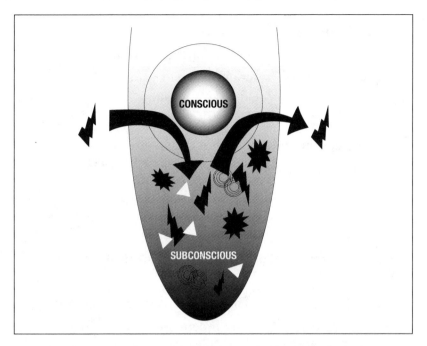

FIGURE 4.1. Push Buttons. Push buttons are formed in the subconscious mind by energy congestions that have not been allowed to fully flow. When they are triggered or "pushed" by a memory, word, or image, they produce an automatic reaction, which can be either distressful or pleasant.

the pain and avoid it. The part of the event that is not fully experienced by the conscious mind sinks into the subconscious mind as an unprocessed or unresolved distress and becomes a push button. It becomes an energy congestion that perpetuates itself due to new distressful energy generated by subsequent experiences that are again not completely processed. Because of the initial push button, there is a tendency to avoid subsequent experiences of the same type, thus reinforcing the previous unresolved distress and evasive behaviors.

If the rational faculty is weak, then the perpetuation of the distressful experience can have a regressive effect, making the psyche withdraw into a self-defensive cocoon. If it is strong, then the withdrawal reaction can be balanced with opposite actions or decisions made by the conscious will, although such a balancing act doesn't erase the push button.

We discuss more thoroughly the nature of the peripheral consciousness, including that of the superconscious or transcendent consciousness, in chapter 6.

The Pervasive Influence of Conditionings

The conditioned subconscious mind is sometimes called the second mind. It is practically independent from the conscious mind. In fact, it is so self-directed that it takes a tremendous effort for the conscious mind to gain back control over the reaction pattern of the subconscious mind.

When we like chocolate ice cream, or dislike people with mustaches, or react with anger to being called fat, we are not reacting from the conscious mind. These are the reactions of the conditioned, subconscious mind. My conscious mind may not want to be afraid of cats because I see how tame and cute they are on the lap of my friend or my sister, but my subconscious mind overrides this conscious realization, and fear takes over my whole organism.

In the case of emotional pain, in which the energy involved in the painful experience is not allowed to flow naturally, the conditioned responses are frozen in the subconscious mind. The energy remains as a congestion in the psycho-physiological system and is triggered automatically every time a stimulus activates it. This is hypothetically true of all kinds of conditionings, but whether we can generalize and extend this hypothesis to all cases remains to be seen.

The influence of conditioning is pervasive and significantly affects ambitions, religious views, philosophy of life, careers, behavior in relationships, and even the smallest things like whether we put socks on the right foot first or the left foot first.

Our worldview is molded by countless influences. The main ones are:

- parents or the people who raised us

- teachers

- television and movies

- peers

- books and magazines

- life experiences

Until we develop self-awareness, we hardly choose our conditionings. For the most part, they simply happen to us. This is particularly so for people whose inner self or inner nature has constantly been suppressed due to fear. But if we are placed in an environment of growth, with ample opportunity for self-discovery, then we may, at an early age, take a more significant part in accepting or rejecting potential conditionings. This is the vital role of an enlightened educational approach.

The Power to Have Mastery over Our Conditionings

Conflicts in conditionings involve the following:

- *One part of personality versus another part of personality*: there are incompatible conditionings in the subconscious mind (the outer self), such as the desire to travel and the fear of flying in airplanes.

- *Higher mind versus part of the personality*: there is a conflict between principles or realities perceived by the higher mind and the interests or needs of the lower personality.

In the first case, the conflict is resolved by extinguishing one of the conditionings. In the second case, it is resolved by strengthening the inner self and changing the conditioning of the outer self by aligning it with the values of the higher mind.

Strengthening the inner nature is the key to mastery over the outer self. We are not simply trying to recondition the habits of the outer, but rather, to make the outer self subservient to the dictates of the inner self.

The third part of the self-transformation process, self-mastery, is devoted to neutralizing undesirable conditionings and forming wholesome ones. Such change is based on clarity about one's values and priorities.

CHAPTER FIVE

Human Perfectibility

In this chapter, we explore the perfectibility of every human being. All individuals are like seeds that have the full potential of the plant locked within them. The harmonious development of one's potential results in self-realization. This state is the culminating point of the ancient and modern spiritual and mystical practices of the world.

We are born imperfect (with the seed of perfection buried deep within), of imperfect parents, within an imperfect society. As a result of these imperfect foundations, we bungle our lives time and again, get wounded physically and psychologically, and frequently feel the sorrow and pain of living.

Fortunately, enough evidence exists that life need not be lived that way. There are human beings—very many of them—who have found the higher realities of life and discovered the keys to ending sorrow, and who have realized the profound potential of a human being, that is, human perfection.

Human perfectibility doesn't mean that we become gods, just as a perfect dog doesn't become a god. It is still a dog, but one that has reached the highest potentials of dogness. But human perfection does mean that we have awakened potentials within ourselves that may make us look superhuman. Thus, we have historical personages such as Gandhi, Christ, Buddha,

Apollonius of Tyana, the Count of St. Germain, St. Francis of Assisi, and others who are regarded with awe and reverence, for they seem to have attained a level of potential and maturity that takes them out of the ordinary.

Modern psychology has, to some extent, recognized this phenomenon. Abraham Maslow refers to such people as self-actualized individuals (although the Eastern concept of perfection goes beyond this concept of Maslow's). Carl Jung calls this maturation process "individuation," in which the individual transcends the ego and realizes the Self.[1] Roberto Assagioli calls it "psychosynthesis," in which the different aspects of consciousness reflect the will of the true Self.[2] Other psychologists have also recognized these levels of maturity that indicate this upward ascent toward perfection, such as Carl Rogers's "fully functioning" individual, Gordon Allport's "functional autonomy," and Alfred Adler's "creative selfhood."

In every case, whether from the mystical or from the psychological point of view, such a realized individual has arrived at a deeper understanding of reality, is clear about the hierarchy of the values in life, has attained self-mastery, and has transcended the normal levels of human consciousness. They have freed themselves from the sorrows and unhappiness that flesh is heir to.

The Qualities of Self-Actualized People

Maslow, more than any other psychologist, conducted extensive studies of these mature and integrated individuals. He saw human beings as characterized by a hierarchy of needs: basic, security, belonging, self-esteem, and self-actualization.

He emphasized the natural tendency of people to ascend to higher needs and the increasing indifference of such people to their lower needs, such as social or physical needs. The needs encountered on the self-actualization level are called meta-needs and constitute the pursuit of such values as truth, beauty, and harmony.

I have summarized below the qualities of the self-actualized individual based on Maslow's writings.[3] These qualities converge toward those traits recognized among self-realized people in spiritual traditions.

- Self-actualized people have *"more efficient perception of reality and more comfortable relations with it."* This means they have a minimum of distortions in their perceptions of people and environment in contradistinction to the neurotic, who is often cognitively wrong. Self-actualized people are more at home with reality and are less threatened by it.

- They are able to *accept themselves* as they are, including their shortcomings and weaknesses. In the same manner, they *accept others*.

- They exhibit a high degree of *spontaneity*. They are not hampered by rigid conventions, and neither are they rebels for rebellion's sake.

- They are *not ego-centered*. Rather, they are occupied with problems or causes outside their own skin. They are *mission oriented*.

- They enjoy *solitude and privacy* and are *detached and unruffled* by events that might upset others.

- They are autonomous and not dependent on culture and environment. They are "dependent for their own development and continued growth upon *their own potentialities and latent resources.*"

- They exhibit a continual *freshness of appreciation.* They repeatedly experience awe and wonder and pleasure in their everyday world.

- They have *mystic experiences* or *oceanic feelings* in which they experience ecstasy, awe, and wonder.

- They have a deep feeling of *compassion* for human beings in general.

- They have *deep interpersonal relations* with others.

- They are *democratic in their attitudes.* They do not discriminate on the basis of class, race, or color.

- They are *highly ethical*; they have a clear sense of right and wrong.

- They have a *healthy, nonhostile sense of humor.*

- They are *creative.* They have a fresh, naive, direct way of looking at things.

Gordon Allport similarly listed the qualities that indicate maturity, which parallel those of Maslow.[4]

Alan Watts, in his *Psychotherapy East and West,* wrote:

Psychotherapy and the ways of liberation have two interests in common: first, the transformation of consciousness, of the inner feeling of one's own existence; and second, the release of the individual from forms of conditioning imposed upon him by social institutions.[5]

In citing the theories of Maslow, Jung, and Assagioli, we must take care that we don't equate them with the concept of perfection in the mystical traditions. In the Buddhist, Indian, and even Christian traditions, the concept of perfection far transcends the admirable maturity that Maslow has described. In the East, perfected beings not only have freed themselves from the cycle of pain and sorrow (*dukha*), but also have attained a level of knowledge and consciousness that brings them closer or more attuned to the fount of existence, what people call the Absolute, God, Reality, or the Divine Life. These people have transcended earthly desires and are liberated from the cycle of necessity or reincarnation. In many such traditions, these great beings have also mastered unknown laws of nature so that they are able to do things regarded as miraculous, as in the cases of Padre Pio, Paramahansa Yogananda, and Therese Neumann.

This quest for human perfection is reflected in many of the classic works of mysticism, not only in Eastern traditions, but also in the Judeo-Christian-Islamic traditions. Hindus refer to such individuals who have reached that goal as *rishis* or *jivan-muktas*, liberated souls. The term *mahatma*, or great soul, is used extensively in theosophical literature. Buddhists refer to them according to their various levels of enlightenment; they include *arhats*, *bodhisattvas*, and *buddhas*. In the Old Testament, they belong to the Order of Melchizedek.[6] The New Testament refers to them as "just men made perfect."[7] St. Teresa of Avila entitled her book on this upward ascent *The Way of Perfection*. Al-Jili, a Muslim Sufi, wrote a book entitled *Al-insan al kamil*, or the Perfect Man. Such personages have not only reached a high level of spiritual attainment, but have resolved many of the fundamental riddles and problems of human life.

One sense of the word *saint* similarly refers to such attainment, but many of those who have been declared saints may only have been martyrs for the Catholic Church rather than self-realized beings.[8]

The Awakening of Higher Consciousness

The path toward perfection always entails the awakening of a higher level of consciousness, not a horizontal, linear expansion of existing states.

Figure 5.1 illustrates that in each kingdom of nature, there is an added level of consciousness that distinguishes it from the preceding one.[9]

LEVEL OF CONSCIOUSNESS	Mineral	Plant	Animal	Human	Perfect Human
Atma					
Buddhi					
Higher Mind					
Lower Mind					
Emotional					
Physical/ Etheric					

FIGURE 5.1. **Kingdoms of Nature**. In each of the so-called kingdoms of nature, note that an essential difference among them is the addition of a quality of consciousness of a higher nature compared to the preceding one.

On Self-Awareness

Self-awareness is the key to the self-transformation process. Coupled with age-old insights about *ch'i* or *pranic* energy, self-awareness can heal emotional wounds and dissipate irrational fears. In its subtler aspects, awareness is the essential element in meditation and the doorway to transcendent consciousness.

An alternative way of understanding consciousness is shown in figure 6.1. It is adapted from a diagram in Roberto Assagioli's *Psychosynthesis*. This idea is analogous to the higher and lower triangle diagram in chapter 3 (figure 3.1), but it highlights a different aspect of consciousness.

The circle at the center of figure 6.1 represents present consciousness and is surrounded by the preconscious level. The preconscious mind is that repository of information and memories that are readily accessible by the conscious mind. It is not the subconscious mind, nor is it in the field of present consciousness. The preconscious mind may also be regarded as a consciousness that is between the conscious and the subconscious minds.

The subconscious mind represents the area in which information and memories are stored with their accompanying emotional energies. A part of the subconscious mind interacts

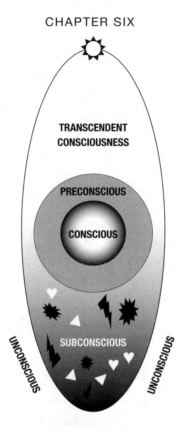

FIGURE 6.1. Human Consciousness. Human consciousness has certain important aspects: the field of conscious attention, the preconscious, the subconscious, and the transcendent consciousness. The push buttons, or conditioned reaction patterns, are found in the subconscious.

easily with the conscious mind. Other parts are not as easily accessible even if they affect the behavior of the person.

The transcendent consciousness, or superconsciousness, is that level equivalent to mystical, spiritual, or intuitive consciousness. It transcends the concrete and abstract thinking levels. The radiant circle at the top in figure 6.1 represents the true Self, equivalent to the spirit, or *atma*. Remember that this is a two-dimensional diagram, and the true Self must not be understood as situated vertically on top of the consciousness.

One's consciousness, or attention, is normally focused on some object or idea. When it is, it tends to be oblivious to other things that are perceived or experienced in the periphery of consciousness, such as the sounds of the surroundings or even a subconscious, emotional reaction to something. (*Subconscious* here means below the normal field of consciousness, not *unconscious*. The subconscious level should be regarded as multilayered, from the periphery of the attention to deep subconsciousness.)

When the attention is focused on something, other perceptions are relegated to the subconscious mind; thus, one doesn't notice a door slam while reading a novel. (But it can be recalled through hypnosis.) This field of attention can be expanded or accompanied by a substratum of semi-attentive consciousness that plays a central role in self-awareness. Figure 6.2 illustrates these distinctions.

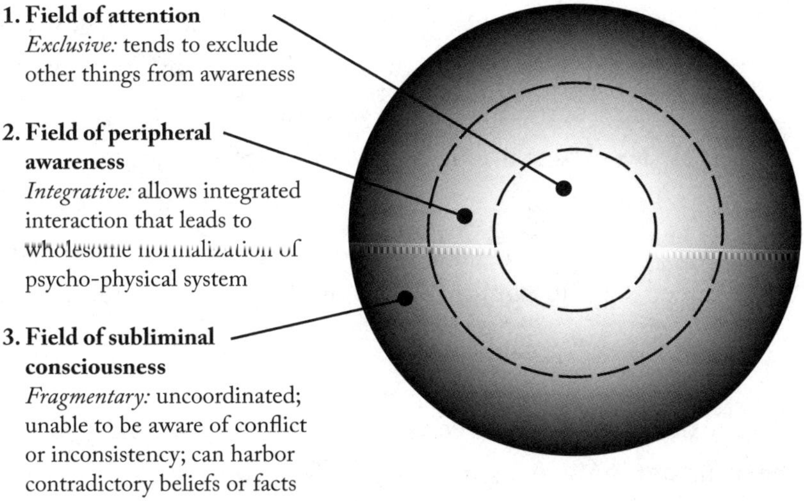

1. Field of attention
Exclusive: tends to exclude other things from awareness

2. Field of peripheral awareness
Integrative: allows integrated interaction that leads to wholesome normalization of psycho-physical system

3. Field of subliminal consciousness
Fragmentary: uncoordinated; unable to be aware of conflict or inconsistency; can harbor contradictory beliefs or facts

FIGURE 6.2. Levels of Consciousness

As figure 6.2 illustrates, consciousness (as opposed to the subconscious and superconscious spheres) can be classified into three levels:

1. The field of attention: This field is the area of consciousness that focuses on objects. It has the quality of being exclusive; that is, it excludes whatever is outside its attention.

2. The field of peripheral awareness: This field is like the penumbra of the field of attention. It possesses the quality of integration; that is, it is aware of contradictions and conflicts in what is perceived or experienced and thus paves the way toward integration. This is discussed more fully in the next section.

3. The field of subliminal consciousness: This field constitutes the parts that don't belong to the first two fields but are still part of the active sphere of consciousness (as contrasted to the subconscious sphere). It has the quality of being fragmented in the way it holds its contents; that is, it absorbs without being aware of contradictions or conflicts. Thus, the contents are left uncoordinated and unintegrated. Its reaction pattern is almost solely influenced by the conditionings of the subconscious mind, hence is automatic.

The field of subliminal consciousness is the dominant part of the minds of individuals who lack self-awareness. It is through this field that subconscious urges and tendencies are carried out or translated into action while we are awake, making us conscious of such actions. (The subconscious mind can directly produce actions while we are asleep, but we are not conscious of them because they do not pass through any of these three fields. It is the involvement of the subliminal consciousness field that makes us conscious of automatic reactions that arise out of the subconscious.)

To be conscious of an action, however, does not mean that the action is produced with self-mastery or self-awareness. Actions that pass through only the subliminal part of consciousness are not integrated with the other parts of the mind. Thus, if I automatically react with fear to a picture of a snake, the reaction is unintegrated with the knowledge or realization that a picture is not dangerous and that there is no need to fear or avoid it. Actions through this field are therefore conditioned, automatic, and may often be irrational.

The Field of Peripheral Awareness

The second layer, the field of peripheral awareness, plays a most crucial role in the development of self-awareness. It is this layer that makes us conscious of an internal conflict, an automatic tendency, a like or dislike, a bias, or an attitude. It gives us the opportunity to review and assess the wisdom of these automatic tendencies or responses of the subconscious mind (through the field of subliminal consciousness). With the expansion of this layer, one becomes more truly in charge of actions and reactions, as compared to the time prior to being aware. One is, in a significant sense, more awake and more capable of making choices. There is greater freedom.

In the average person, this peripheral awareness is dim and narrow. In many types of neuroses, it is extremely narrow, and in countless psychotics it is effectively nonfunctional. Psychotics are virtually prisoners of their conditioned reaction patterns. They are not free to make intelligent and conscious choices because they are hardly aware of any. They just react automatically and hence involuntarily.

The field of peripheral awareness can be expanded or deepened through meditation and daily exercise of self-awareness. A larger and more diffused field of peripheral awareness can include an awareness of bodily reactions, fear reactions, irritation, motivations, likes and dislikes, thoughts, opinions, and attitudes.

The *content* of this field of peripheral awareness is *consciously processed* almost immediately by the field of attention, whereas the content in the outer field of subliminal consciousness will be *automatically* dealt with by conditionings with very little or no awareness. This point is important for self-mastery, because conflicts or inconsistencies can be more effectively dealt with when we are aware of them than when we are not.

Another reason for the significance of an active and expanded field of peripheral awareness is that because conflicts are attended to immediately, they don't contribute to the accumulated psychological baggage in the subconscious mind. Conflicts are dealt with and resolved as they occur. They are not suppressed or evaded. If they are unresolved, such an unresolved state is consciously recognized rather than shoved into the subconscious mind. This capacity is an extremely important factor in sustaining the psychological health of an individual.

Emotions and Self-Awareness

Psychological studies affirm that emotions are usually accompanied by physiological reactions or states. Thus, when we are afraid, our bodies are *never* relaxed; they are tense. This tension means that there is a *surging* of energy and the *holding* of that energy somewhere.

When there is no self-awareness, this surging and holding of energy may continue for an extended period, even when danger is no longer present. This is the origin of recurrent psychological distresses such as fear, grief, resentment, and hurt. When caused by a life-threatening experience, the surging and holding can lead to psychological problems such as post-traumatic stress disorder. When there is self-awareness, however, this surging action diminishes to a plateau, and the tension caused by the holding or freezing is relaxed, thus allowing the natural release of the held energy.

This is a vital key to the resolution of emotional problems and conditionings that are the overwhelming causes of human unhappiness and misery. It involves an understanding of the dynamics of the energy that is involved in emotional distress.

The Energy

What is the energy that is held in the body? It is the same energy as the *ch'i* (or *qi*) that travels through the acupuncture meridians in the body. When we are threatened, there is an upsurge of this *ch'i*, and the organism holds on to it while the threat or danger is present. This reaction very likely has a biological root, one that is also found in animals.

Because of our psychological makeup, we dwell on the threat even when it is no longer there. Thus, the holding or freezing of the energy tends to continue. *It sinks to a deeper level in the system in a dormant but ready state.* Thus, when the threat reappears, either actually or in memory, the surging and freezing of the energy recur instantly and automatically.

Understanding this process is the key to removing unwanted irrational emotional reactions such as fear, anger, resentment, and jealousy. When this stored energy is allowed to flow naturally, the automatic reaction of fear or anger disappears with it. This is the process by which irrational reactions disappear when a person undergoes self-awareness processing, which is discussed later.

Abdominal Breathing

What is the role of deep breathing in self-awareness? Abdominal breathing is effective in activating *ch'i* in various parts of the body, including those that are connected with fears and traumas. *When the surge of energy is accompanied by self-awareness, there is no holding or freezing action, allowing the energy to flow to its natural points of release such as the fingers, toes, crown, mouth, and eyes.*

The flow of the *ch'i* is experienced as needlepoints, numbness, trembling, pressure, pain, or warmth. The hands and the fingers, for example, feel the sensation that people describe as electricity, or a tingling sensation. When the energy is strong, the feeling turns to numbness or trembling.

A person undergoing this process must allow the energy to flow naturally until it equilibrates and returns to normalcy. This may take from ten minutes to more than an hour, depending on the intensity of the energy locked up. If the energy is excessive, deep breathing should be discontinued after an hour (the person usually feels tired or exhausted by then) and breathing at a normal rate resumed.

It is important that, in ending a session, there should be no experience of pain or pressure, such as a headache. Otherwise, the breathing should be continued until the pain or pressure subsides. This is to prevent any unnecessary hanging pain that may last for hours or even days when left unresolved in the middle of a process.

The Process

When I speak of *the process* or *to process* something, I am referring to the act of self-awareness accompanied by abdominal breathing being applied to specific frozen energies in a person's psyche and body—a fear, a resentment, a hurt, a painful memory, a trauma, depression, and so on.

The process can be done by yourself if you are familiar with it. For those unfamiliar, it should be done with another person facilitating, one who is experienced in the process. This process is more fully described in succeeding chapters.

Effects of Awareness

The expansion of awareness has certain direct effects upon a person. Below are some benefits of the practice of daily self-awareness:

Body

- Awareness enables us to deal with pain more effectively. Pain is a protective mechanism of the body. It is not an enemy, but an ally. When there is awareness, we experience the pain without feeling miserable.

- It enables us to be more in touch with the needs of the body and to respond to it more effectively. Self-awareness helps us to see the conditioned desires or impulses we have for certain types of food or drink and thereby handle them consciously.

- It can prevent chronic tension or stress.

Emotion

- Awareness can effectively handle distressful emotions such as fear, anger, resentment, attachment, hurt, and depression.

Thinking

- Awareness brings about clarity in thinking.

- It clarifies values.

- It helps us become more objective in our judgment.

- It helps us develop attentive thinking, that is, thinking with awareness, not just with concentration.

Creativity

Because of our awareness of conditionings, prejudgments, and assumptions, our minds become more capable of exploring new directions, thus enhancing creativity.

Intuition

In addition to awareness of the layers of the mind, including feelings and thoughts, we become more aware of the higher level of perception, that is, intuition. We begin to see beyond appearances. Perception becomes more deeply integrated, incorporating deeper spiritual values.

Transcendence

Such an intuitive perception is the beginning of the spiritual or mystical life.

Knowledge versus Awareness

Many people who undergo self-awareness processing often find it difficult to distinguish between knowing and being aware, between knowing and experiencing. They frequently assume that when they know they are angry, it means they are aware that they are angry. This isn't necessarily so. I have observed this difficulty even among those who have gone through the process many times and who have been told about the distinction between knowledge and awareness. We must therefore dwell deeper into this aspect.

Knowledge is a translation of an experience, a symbolization on another level. It is a recording of a thing that has happened and hence is always of the past. Awareness is of the present. It is not a translation, but rather an experiencing.

Knowledge about something involves *naming* it and *classifying* it according to some prearranged categories in the mind, based on a set of information *about* it. When I see an object for the first time, say a cellular phone, I want to know what it is called and what its functions and uses are. I may press the keys and call somebody and feel the exhilaration of the novel experience. Once I have learned this, my mind stores it in its memory bank. The next time I see the same object, this stored information will be retrieved, and I recognize the cellular phone.

Repeated familiarity with it brings this set of information into a subtler, conceptual level such that when I see the cellular phone, my mind almost subconsciously recognizes it without my having to recall the name and the detailed functions of it. This is true for things like chairs, pens, houses, clouds, and a million other things, including people and subjective experiences such as anger and hurt. When we recognize those things in this way, we are drawing upon the memory data bank on a conceptual level but not experiencing the object as we did in the beginning. This recognition therefore is indirect and symbolic. It is not an experience of the object, but a recognition, because of its identity with a particular set of data in the memory. This recognition is automatic and happens so fast that we don't take note of its dynamics anymore.

This faculty of the mind is extremely useful. But it is also this same faculty that eventually becomes a barrier to the capacity to experience things in the present moment. We now confuse knowing and experiencing.

When I am angry, I will probably recognize its symptoms in me, such as shouting at people. I *know* I am angry, but I am not necessarily aware of my state of anger. I may not be aware, for example, that I am clenching my fist, my head is physically hot, my jaws are tight or tense, and my heart is thumping hard. All these are part of the experience of anger at this moment. An angry person is usually unaware of these experiential elements of the anger, which are just happening automatically.

To be in touch with these aspects of anger is the beginning of awareness. As I have said, they are not without purpose. Awareness brings back the mastery over conditioned reaction patterns in the psyche that cause conflicts and problems.

Awareness has degrees. Its scope varies, depending on the extent to which the consciousness encompasses aspects of an experience. For example, in anger, I may be aware of the loudness of my voice but not my clenched fist. Or I may be aware of my clenched fist but not the mental-emotional prejudice or prejudgment that has arisen in my mind and triggered the anger. The larger the field of peripheral awareness, the more we are aware of. This peripheral awareness, however, is not something we can easily expand at will. It is a quality of consciousness brought about by nurture and practice. Conscious breathing, self-awareness processing, and meditation are practices that help expand peripheral awareness.

Awareness is an experience of a direct phenomenon and is not interpreted by the mind. An unpleasant "pain" is already an interpretation, a second-level experience. The first-level experience is an awareness of a sensation produced by the nerves sending signals to the brain. In its raw form, the experience is just that—a sensation that emanates from a certain location in the body. Psychologically, it is neither pleasant nor unpleasant, even though the body is automatically reacting to the message from the nerves.

Am I in Pain?

An exercise called "Am I in Pain?" illustrates the concept discussed in the previous section. I suggest you do the exercise as you read so the subsequent discussion will be meaningful. It takes one to two minutes.

First, pinch yourself hard on the inside part of your upper

arm. It is probably unpleasant, and you may not like the experience. Then do it a second time, but this time with a difference. First, touch your skin without pinching. Go into deep breathing while feeling the touch of your fingers on your inner arm. Then slowly press your fingers in a pinching manner, but not hard. Feel the sensation. Be aware of any experience connected with the pressing of the fingers. Then press a little harder. Do this slowly. Feel whether the sensation is spreading to the other parts of the arm. If so, just experience it fully. Slowly press harder and harder, and finally press as hard as you can while still experiencing the entire sensation fully. After two to three seconds of pinching yourself hard, let go. When you have finished, rub the skin where you pinched yourself so it doesn't turn blue.

What is the difference between the first and second time you pinched yourself? The first occasion was probably painful and you probably didn't like it. How about the second time? Did you feel miserable or distressed?

Many people who have gone through this exercise said the first pinching was "painful" but the second one was not. Take note of this paradox. In the second pinching, you were, in fact, fully experiencing what was supposed to be "pain," and yet, strange but true, it wasn't pain as you usually know it. You experienced the sensation and the way it spread to other parts of the skin or arm. You weren't avoiding the sensation, yet it wasn't unpleasant. Awareness brings us to a first level of experience rather than to a second or third level of experience (such as the psychological reaction of unpleasantness) or to a mere knowledge about the experience.

Awareness in Meditation

When we practice meditation, the observations discussed in the previous section become more important. Awareness of thoughts is different from thinking about thoughts. The latter involves recognition, naming, and classifying; we label the thoughts as "disturbances" or "intrusions." Thinking about thoughts is the second level of experiencing thoughts, which is different from being aware of thoughts. Thinking about thoughts pigeonholes them into types and categories: wanted and unwanted, desirable and undesirable. These all come from the data bank of the memory. It is not direct awareness. We may now better appreciate why J. Krishnamurti refers to such direct, raw awareness as "choiceless awareness." It is an awareness without judgment, preference, analysis, discrimination, or even naming.

This nonjudgmental awareness is not the same as the blank awareness of an infant who has not yet learned to name or classify. The latter is an open state that absorbs and helps develop new neural connections. The experience of the former is absorbed by an inner level of the consciousness that is nonlogical but more intuitive. It has a wisdom of its own that transcends the discursive and analytical mind. It is what Buddhists call *prajna*, the contemplative consciousness of the Christian mystics. Therefore, this non-opinionated awareness is not just a blank absorption of things. It has a noetic value that is different from intellectual knowing. William James refers to such noetic perceptions as "states of insights into depths of truth unplumbed by the discursive intellect. They are illuminations, revelations, full of significance and importance, all inarticulate though they may remain; and as a rule they carry with them a curious sense of authority."[1] We often don't recognize this, because intellectual recognition is the only knowing that we usually understand.

Awareness and Transcendence

What we are aware of, we transcend. When we are aware of physical pain, we transcend the pain while experiencing it. Awareness is beyond or more than the pain. It is a larger holon, so to speak, that includes pain but is not limited by or exclusively identified with it. (See the discussion of holons in chapter 27.)

When we are aware of emotional distress, we transcend it. The same principle applies to thoughts, conditionings, concepts, perceptions, and the self. True awareness, therefore, is the key to freedom. It allows us to be free from spheres of experience or structures of consciousness that imprison us. Self-awareness is like an imprisoned person who turns into an invisible, expanding mist that can pass through the walls of the prison. Ultimate awareness is beyond this mist. It is neither expanding nor imprisoned. There is no prison and no prisoner.

Guidelines on Self-Awareness Processing

Self-awareness, coupled with abdominal breathing, is the basic tool for working out the removal of unwholesome conditioning. Self-awareness processing can be done by yourself alone (auto-processing), or it can be done with the help of another person. Eventually, self-awareness processing should be done by yourself alone. At the beginning, however, it is very helpful to undergo the process with the help of a facilitator or guide.

Abdominal Breathing

Abdominal breathing is an important part of self-awareness processing. It intensifies the flow of *ch'i* through the entire system, particularly the meridians, because it activates the *tan t'ien* (*hara* in Japanese) center in the abdominal area, which is said to be the repository of *ch'i*. Through such breathing, any existing congestion will be felt more palpably because of the temporary pressure created by the intensified movement of *ch'i*. Self-awareness allows the channels to loosen and relax, thus allowing the congestion to release and flow.

This is the procedure for abdominal breathing (see figure 8.1):

- Put your palms on your abdomen about two inches below the navel.

- Move your palms forward and backward by expanding and contracting the muscles of your abdomen.

- Next, expand the abdomen and breathe in through your nose, then expand your diaphragm and your chest.

- When you exhale, blow the air out through your mouth and contract your abdominal muscles.

- Take about five seconds to inhale and another five seconds to exhale. One way of keeping track of five seconds is by mentally counting at a steady pace: "one thousand one, one thousand two, one thousand three, one thousand four, one thousand five."

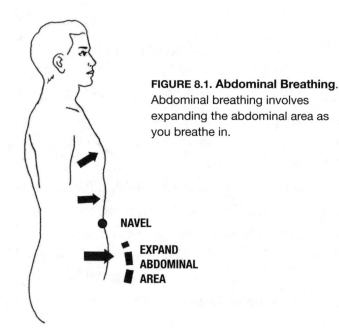

FIGURE 8.1. Abdominal Breathing. Abdominal breathing involves expanding the abdominal area as you breathe in.

NAVEL

EXPAND
ABDOMINAL
AREA

Abdominal breathing is actually natural breathing. If we watch babies breathe while they are sleeping, we notice that it is their bellies that heave up and down.

Once you have learned abdominal breathing, you are ready for the next step, which is scanning. Scanning has a triple purpose. First, it allows you to be aware of existing surface tension or congestion in your body and to let these tensions relax. Second, it makes you aware of the difference between tension or congestion and true relaxation. This awareness is not only important in processing, but vitally necessary for daily living. And finally, scanning prepares you for the more intensive emotional processing that comes later.

The guidelines below are divided into two parts: processing yourself and processing others. The procedures are identical, but there are special considerations when we are processing another person. When we are processing ourselves, we know what is happening to us, but when we are processing others, we only know what the person tells us or what we see in the expressions in the face and body.

Processing Yourself: Self-Scanning

The procedure for scanning yourself is as follows:

- Sit in a comfortable position, with both feet flat on the floor and both hands on your lap with palms faced upward. Do abdominal breathing at least five times before starting to scan. Continue the deep abdominal breathing throughout the entire session. Close your eyes (although this can be done with eyes open, if preferred).

- As you breathe in the sixth time, be aware of the crown. Feel or sense any sensation there. See whether you feel any heaviness, tension, pressure, or pain. Do two breathing cycles while being aware of the crown.

- If you feel heaviness, tension, or pain in the crown, then be aware of the nature of the sensation. Is it a small area or a large area? Is it pulsating, or is it a constant pressure? Is it a circular area, or is it a line? If it is a line, how thick is it? By taking note of these qualities, you *experience* the tension rather than *think about* the tension.

- As you breathe in, experience the tension or heaviness. As you breathe out, feel the back of your neck, your shoulders, your back, and your arms and hands. (The sequence of awareness while breathing in and out will depend on the natural direction of the flow of *ch'i* in the body. Thus, if the congestion is in the throat, then at the outbreath one must be aware of the mouth and jaw.)

- Do not try to fight or change the tension. Just be aware of it, or experience it fully, as you breathe in and out. Do this until the heaviness or pain dissipates.

- You may feel heaviness on your shoulders or arms. Be aware of such heaviness. It may even turn into numbness or a tingling sensation in the fingers. Be aware of these too as you breathe out.

- If your head doesn't feel any tension or discomfort, then move on to the forehead and eyes. Follow the same procedure as above if you feel any heaviness or tension. If none, then move to the face and jaw. Then scan the neck and shoulder areas, the chest, the stomach and abdominal area, the arms and hands, the back, the hips, and finally, the legs and feet.

- If you feel any discomfort at any part of the body, process that area.

- After processing any tension, heaviness, pain, or numbness, scan your body again and check whether there is still any tension or discomfort anywhere. If there is, then go through the process again.

- If you had muscular pains prior to your scanning, include such pains in your scanning.

- The scanning session is complete after you feel completely relaxed. If you had tensions or pains that were released while scanning, you may feel tired afterward.

Emotional Processing

Once you have done the scanning properly, you are ready to process emotional conflicts. This is essentially the same as scanning, except that you will now think of a person or event that has angered, hurt, or upset you. If you are not yet very familiar with scanning, the emotional processing is best done with the help of a facilitator or guide.

The procedure for self-processing is as follows:

- Sit comfortably as in scanning; do abdominal breathing at least five times.

- Scan the body, whether it is relaxed or not. If not, then go through the scanning process until your entire body is completely relaxed.

- After your body is relaxed, think of a person or incident that has angered, hurt, or upset you. Remember to continue deep abdominal breathing throughout the session.

- If the remembered episode remains an unresolved emotional issue, then you are likely to feel something in your body as you breathe deeply. It can be a heaviness or a pain in the chest, a head pressure, back pain, or some discomfort in other parts of the body. (If you don't feel anything, it doesn't necessarily mean that the issue has been resolved within you. The self-defensive ego may have taken charge, preventing you from being in touch with deeper layers of your consciousness.)

- If you feel something, then process it as you did in scanning. Do it until the congestion normalizes. It may take five minutes or sixty minutes, but generally it normalizes within ten minutes or so.

- After the heaviness or pressure is gone, check your entire body for any remaining tension. Process any tension or discomfort that you notice.

- When your body is fully relaxed, then recall again the same person or episode. If there is again a reaction of discomfort, process it again as above.

- After reaching relaxation and checking for any remaining tension, recall the incident again. Do this till there is no longer any reaction of discomfort.

- If you have been doing the processing with your eyes closed, then do it now with your eyes open. If you still feel any discomfort, process it again.

- Scan your entire body for any tension before ending the session. Your whole body should be relaxed, even though you may feel tired.

In doing the above procedure, you may feel drained or tired after the first round. If you feel like resting, then do so after you have reached full relaxation. If you don't feel too tired, continue with a second round, then a third, or until there is no unpleasant reaction to the memory anymore.

Helping Others to Process Themselves

The guidelines in the last section are for self-processing. We now turn our attention to the guidelines for helping others process themselves.

When you help others in self-awareness processing, it usually means that the other person is not yet familiar with the method. It is common for the person to not understand the instructions or not follow them correctly. They may also resist the instructions, especially if there is pain. Therefore, as a facilitator or guide, you play an important role in the success of the processing. You must know how to ask the proper questions and be sensitive to the body language of the person to know what is happening internally. You must know how to direct the breathing and awareness procedure to help the flow of *ch'i* and decongest the system. You must also be experienced enough not to be alarmed by seemingly intense sensations or pains, and you must know how to handle them. People who know how to process themselves are not necessarily ready to process others. Training and experience are required.

Caution

If you have attended the Self-Transformation Seminar, you were cautioned about processing the emotions of other people unless you have been adequately prepared and asked to do so. Some people may go through intense emotional reactions, such as severe phobias, traumatic memories, and intense guilt, and it takes an experienced facilitator to handle these extreme cases. Gain more experience with auto-processing first. Or, if you have the opportunity, participate in seminars where you can serve as an assistant facilitator under the guidance of a more experienced facilitator.

Scanning Another Person

The procedure for scanning another person is the same as the guidelines on self-scanning, except that you are now facilitating the processing of another person.

- Sit facing the subject without touching one another. The feet of the subject should be flat on the floor, with both hands on the lap, palms upward. Ask the subject to do abdominal breathing at least five times. Observe whether it is being done correctly. If not, then ask the subject to blow the air out so that you can feel the exhaled air if you put your hand about one and a half feet away from the subject's face.

- Ask the subject to be aware of the crown and the back of the head. Pause for ten seconds. Then ask whether there is any feeling of discomfort there. (Make sure that the person understands "discomfort." You may say: "Is there any tension, heaviness, pressure, or pain in the top and back part of your head?") Pause again and wait for an answer.

- If the subject says that something is felt, such as, "There's a pain in my head," then ask, "Which part?" Let the subject completely experience the sensation by asking specific questions, helping the person to be aware of the size of the sensation, its thinness or thickness, hardness or softness, the intensity, sharpness or dullness, and so on. Helpful questions are, "How large is the area of the pain? What is the shape of the pain? Is it hard or soft?"

- If the pain has subsided, then ask about other areas. If the person voluntarily says that there is a sensation or pain in a specific area such as the chest, then go ahead and process the chest pain.

- All throughout the scanning session, observe any change in the expression of the subject's face or movement of the body. There may be some indications about what the person is feeling inside. Some examples of things to take note of include knotting the eyebrows, tapping the fingers, or pressing the lips. These usually indicate tension or discomfort. They belie verbal statements that the subject is already relaxed.

- Remember that when there is congestion or pain in one area, ask the subject to feel it fully when breathing in and feel the surrounding or downflow area when exhaling. The exception is when the congestion, heaviness, or numbness is felt in the hands or feet; then let the subject feel it while exhaling. (As mentioned above, the sequence of awareness while breathing in and out depends upon the natural direction of the flow of *ch'i* in the body.)

- When you notice an inner struggle, remind the subject not to fight or change the tension, but just to be aware of it, or to experience it fully, while breathing in and out. Do this until the heaviness or pain dissipates naturally.

- When the subject feels that the pressure or discomfort has dissipated, ask the subject again to check the entire body and see whether there is still any other discomfort. If there is any, then process it again. Take note that when the person claims to be already relaxed, you must still check whether this is true by observing the facial expression and body posture.

- Only after the person feels completely relaxed is the scanning session completed.

Facilitating Emotional Processing

The procedure for facilitating the emotional processing of a subject is as follows:

- Have the person go through scanning to ensure that the body is fully relaxed. If some discomfort emerges from the scanning, process it until the person relaxes. Do not proceed to emotional scanning until the person is fully relaxed. Full relaxation enables the person to become sensitive to the presence of discomfort. (However, if the person has already thought of some painful memories and is already experiencing physical discomfort when you start the session, then proceed with the emotional processing since there is no other choice.)

- With eyes closed, ask the subject to recall a person or incident that has upset or angered or hurt him or her. Pause twenty seconds.

- Ask the subject if there is any sensation or discomfort in the body. Proceed to process any discomfort in the body until the discomfort normalizes.

- In receiving replies from the subject, take note of vague, conceptual, or nonspecific answers. A statement like, "I feel hurt" is not a *description* of what is being experienced but a *concept* of what is felt. Ask, "Where do you feel it in your body?" Skillful questions help the subject become *aware* of the experience, rather than tell you what *they think* about the experience. These are two very different things. Hence, asking about size, hardness, or thickness, for example, helps the person to *be aware* rather than *to think* or *conceptualize* about what is being experienced.

- Process until all discomfort normalizes.

- If the person is not yet too tired, repeat the procedure by asking the subject to recall the incident for a second time. If there is still some discomfort or heaviness or pain, no matter how slight, then go through the process again until the discomfort normalizes. Repeat the processing cycle until nothing is felt anymore when recalling the incident.

- There will come a point when the person no longer has any adverse reaction to the memory. In some cases, the person may state that he or she misses or loves the person the subject previously thought was hated (such as a father).

- Ask the subject to open his or her eyes and to think once more of the other person. If there is still an uncomfortable reaction, then go through the processing once more.

Further Guidelines for Processing

The commentaries in this chapter are for individuals who are helping other people going through the self-awareness process. Where relevant, the notes also apply to people who are doing auto-processing, that is, those who process themselves without the help of another person.

Physical Aspects

Here are some of the physical aspects of the processing session:

- Sit facing the subject. Your knees should not touch the subject's legs. Hence, if necessary, sit a little to one side of the subject to be able to be nearer and hear the person better.

- Avoid touching the subject. Although touching at appropriate times can help convey your empathy, especially when the subject is undergoing strong emotional experiences, touching can also make the subject feel guarded or uncomfortable. In certain cultures, touching is very inappropriate.

- Look at the subject and observe what is happening at all times. There may be times when you need to process yourself to be aware of what is happening within you. But this should not prevent you from being alert to what is going on in the subject. For this reason, avoid writing anything while processing the other person.

Verbal Communication

The main mode of communication during the session is verbal. Here are a few reminders on this aspect:

- Your voice, manner, and tone of speaking play important roles in the processing. It is from the voice that the feeling of trust is conveyed. When you are anxious, such anxiety is conveyed through the voice. Be conscious about your own tension and whether you are speaking in a high-pitched voice, which can indicate lack of relaxation.

- During the processing, the questions you ask shouldn't be too intrusive, such as asking too many questions too often. The subject will be distracted from self-awareness. The questions should be based on what you feel is needed at that moment.

- Neither should there be too few questions or reminders. A subject not very familiar with the self-awareness processing is likely to go into brooding or recollecting, rather than attaining a state of self-awareness. Your questions or reminders are meant to bring back awareness to the physico-etheric experiences in the body.

- Ask "what" questions and do not ask "why" questions. "What" questions ask for factual descriptions of an experience; "why" questions make the subject go into mentation and justification, which tend to draw the subject away from self-awareness.

- In helping others to process, avoid suggestive reminders, except the reminder to breathe and to be aware. For example, don't suggest to the subject that they should "be relaxed." Avoid suggestions that aim to assure or make the person feel positive, such as, "You'll feel better," or "You'll feel good after this." The purpose of the processing is to help the person become aware without being judgmental.

Duration of the Session

How long a processing session lasts varies according to the circumstance. Here are some pointers:

- The duration of the processing session may range from fifteen minutes to two hours, depending on the subject. Some people are able to go through the process very quickly. Others may find the energy in the body moving to and fro without flowing out, even after an hour.

- See to it that there are no feelings of discomfort, tension, or pain left at the end of each session. If the subject still feels a ball at the pit of the stomach, have the person go through the process again until the ball dissolves or moves. Don't become anxious to try dissolve it by hurrying it up. Such haste can sometimes obstruct the process.

- If the subject still feels tightness or tension after a long while, and if it is advisable to discontinue, ask the person to breathe normally and not deeply while still going through self-awareness. The decrease in the energy will lessen the tightness being experienced, yet still allow any remaining tightness to flow through the subject's awareness.

- If there are tensions in some parts of the body that seem not to flow after a long while, such as the head, neck, shoulders, or arms, you may suggest that the subject press certain parts of the body to help the energy flow. It is best that you ask the subject to do it alone, although it may be helpful to demonstrate how to do it.

Pressing tension points: If there are parts of the body that feel painful, heavy, or tight when doing the scanning, pressing these points with the fingers while doing the abdominal breathing can often be very helpful in accelerating the release of the congestion.

For example, when there is headache on the forehead or the crown or the back of the head, try pressing the hollow areas on the sides of the nape. Usually hard balls can be felt that are painful when pressed. Breathe in and feel the headache, and while breathing out, press these balls or painful areas on the nape with the fingers. Press hard and move the fingers in a circular manner. Such massaging movements will help loosen the congestion. Do this for many breathing cycles until the pain subsides. Then press the inner edges of the eyebrows while breathing out, if desired.

When the pain is on the sides of the crown, find these painful areas and press them with the fingers while breathing out.

When the pain is in a temple, then look for the painful part in one of the four corners of the temple (up, down, front, back) and press and rotate the fingers while breathing out.

When the pain or discomfort is on the shoulders, then look for the points on the shoulders that feel painful when pressed. Press them hard with the fingers (again, rotating the fingers) while breathing out. Feel the pain, and do not resist it. Resisting the pain will obstruct the natural flow of the *ch'i*. These painful areas correspond to acupuncture points of the body.

There are two areas that should not be pressed with the fingers. One is the spine itself, and the second is the area below the rib cage where the organs are exposed.

Energy Flow

When the subject goes through abdominal breathing, the congestions in the system receive greater pressure from the flow of *ch'i*, and tension, tightness, or pain may be felt in those areas that are congested. Such constrictions prevent the energy from flowing freely. Awareness prevents constriction of those parts. Figure 9.1 shows major directions of flow during processing, but there are other minor ones.

Your role in aiding the energy to flow naturally is to help the

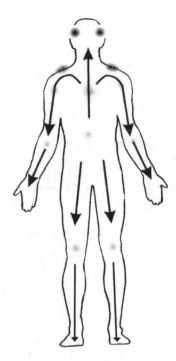

FIGURE 9.1. Directions of Energy Flow. During scanning, some areas in the body, such as the shoulders, chest, or back, may feel tight, heavy, or painful. After the breathing process, they tend to disperse and flow, usually through the extremities.

subject become aware of the area of congestion as indicated by tension, tightness, or pain. In doing this, make use of a number of approaches to identify and be aware of the congested areas:

- Ask about the size: Is it large or small? From what part to what part?

- Ask about the shape: Is it flat? Is it a ball? Is it a line? Rectangle? Oblong?

- Ask about the location: Is it near the surface of the skin? Deep inside?

- Ask about the texture: Is it hard or soft? Is it a sharp or dull pain?

Ask the subject to be aware of the edges of the sensation: for example, if it is a tightness of the chest, ask the person to be aware of the outer edges of the tension, which may be one side of the chest near the upper arm.

Ask the subject to be aware of the area where you think the energy might naturally flow to. If the tension is around the scalp, then ask the subject to be aware of the back of the neck and shoulders, for these are the natural channels of flow of energy from the head. If the tension is on an upper arm, then ask the person to be aware of the forearm and hands.

Common outlets for the flow of the congested energy are the arms, hands, and fingers; the legs, feet, and toes; and the crown of the head.

There have been cases where people reported that the energy went out of their ears, nose, or nipples, but these are rare. There are also occasions when the congestions seem to disappear midway in the body without the subject noticing whether the energy went through any of the above outlets.

Several kinds of sensations are felt when the energy is flowing out. These include:

- a tingling sensation, usually in the extremities. This indicates the free flow of strong energy. It is sometimes described as being pricked by needles or pins.

- numbness, usually the sensation when the energy is very strong. Continue with the awareness of these numb parts, and it will dissipate naturally.

- warmth, usually in the extremities. This indicates the normal flow or release of energy.

- coldness, usually in the hands or feet. This indicates that the energy is flowing but is blocked at some point, such as the wrist or forearm, and the hands feel cold. In this case, it is helpful to ask the subject to be aware of the parts of the body *next to* the cold part. For example, if it is the hands that feel cold, then ask the subject to be aware of the wrist.

- muscular contraction. There are rare times when the energy is so strong that the muscles of the hands contract and harden, and the hand forms into a fist, as if tightly gripping something. Massaging the forearm and hand will help normalize this condition.

Congestions

When abdominal breathing is started with awareness, the subject feels tension, tightness, or pain in those areas where there are congestions in the system. The location of these congestions will vary according to the nature and origin of the emotional problem.

For example, emotions that involve suppression of expression often create congestion in the throat, jaw, or mouth area. Thus, if a child suppresses crying or shouting while being punished by a parent, or when a person suppresses the urge to speak out, the suppression is often felt as a lump in the throat. It will sometimes be felt as a freezing of the jaws, as if the jaws are locked or numb.

Fear, on the other hand, may be felt in the pit of the

stomach. When a fear is recalled, it may appear as a ball around the stomach. It can be hard or soft, large or small. During processing, the size and texture will change. Fear will also be felt in the extremities, such as the legs when there is a fear of heights.

Sensations in or around the eyes often indicate suppressed tears from the past. Anger is felt in several areas of the head, for example, the forehead or the back of the head. Pain in the back area can indicate incomplete flow of the energy from the head. Guilt is felt in the center of the chest. Hurts and resentments are often felt on the center, left, or right side of the chest. They feel like pressure on the heart, resulting in some difficulty in breath. Pressures or heavy responsibilities are felt on the shoulders or back.

Congestions are sometimes felt on one side of the body only, such as the left side of the head and left arm. Rather than being related to the hemispheres of the brain, this seems to be connected to the meridians that flow on one side of the body, from the head downward. Research is going on all the time, and facilitators and those who undergo processing are encouraged to contribute their experiences and observations to deepen our understanding of processing.

Pain

When suppressed emotions are intense, congestion may be felt as pain when the abdominal breathing starts. The pain may be felt in any part of the body, from the head to the extremities, depending on the nature of the emotion and congestion. When it is in the head, for example, the facilitator should guide the subject's awareness to enable the congestion to flow. If the pain is on the forehead or above the eyebrows, then guide the subject to be aware of the temples and sides of the head, then the back of the neck and shoulders.

Acupuncture Meridians

Being familiar with acupuncture meridians or channels through which *ch'i* flows in the body is helpful, because you can then identify the direction of flow and help the subject become aware of the next meridian to prevent obstruction. For example, figure 9.2 illustrates the points of the so-called *stomach meridian* that flows from the sides of the head toward the back of the neck. When there is pain on these areas of the head, then the facilitator should help the subject become aware of the back of the neck during the outbreath cycle.

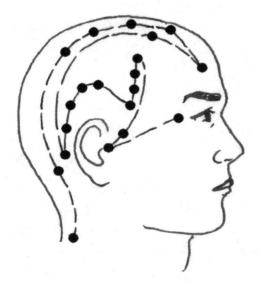

FIGURE 9.2. Meridian Points. This illustration indicates some acupuncture meridians in the head that indicate where the *ch'i* energy tends to either flow or get blocked.

There are fourteen main meridians used in acupuncture; there are also minor meridians as well as connecting links between the meridians. The transfer of sensations of the congestion doesn't follow exactly the points of a specific meridian. The sensations may transfer from one meridian to another or even skip meridian points.

Emotional Effects on the Facilitator

Some facilitators find that when they help process another person, they feel affected when the other person is crying, or feel tired after some time. When we're emotionally affected, we will find ourselves unable to be alert to what is happening to the subject. In fact, we may even find that we are more involved in processing ourselves than in helping the subject. How do we avoid being affected or tired when we are assisting someone?

Being affected by the grief or emotions of another indicates that a push button has been triggered within us. It means that we need to work on something ourselves, later. In the meantime, we must be aware of what is happening to us at that moment, even while we are helping the other person.

When we feel tired after a session with a person, it means that we were not relaxed and calm during the session; we were not aware that we had been tensing a part of the body all the while. The ability to quickly distinguish between tension and relaxation is therefore a necessary capacity that every facilitator must develop.

Awareness and Brooding

The facilitator must take care that the subject doesn't get into brooding or imagination; otherwise, the trauma of the memory is intensified. By asking timely and appropriate questions about physical feelings, the facilitator helps the subject maintain awareness of bodily energies and hence allow the energy to flow naturally. This enables the subject to let go and release pent-up emotions and energies safely and permanently.

Helpful and Unhelpful Behaviors

Here are a few more important reminders:

- As mentioned earlier, when helping subjects process themselves, give your full presence and focused attention to them. Avoid writing or taking notes during the processing, except for writing down the sequence of the process in a body chart.

- Be aware of your own physical body while the subject is undergoing his or her own feelings and sensations. It can help you sense or feel the nature of what the person is feeling.

- When the subject is undergoing emotional pain and is crying, it is sometimes helpful to hold or touch the person's arms or shoulder. Note that this should be done with consideration to its appropriateness. When unsure, avoid it.

Processing between Marital Partners, Relatives, or Friends

In self-awareness processing—particularly emotional processing—couples, relatives, or close friends trying to help process
each other may encounter some difficulties. For example, when
the issue being processed is directly or indirectly related to their
own relationship, there may be a feeling on the part of one
party that the issue is not being addressed and that the processing is an avoidance of the issue. The person who feels hurt
or angry may not even be willing to do the processing. It may
be best to discuss the matter first and then do the processing
after both parties feel that it will be helpful. For unobstructed
mutual processing, there must be no negative emotional issues
between the partners.

Body Movements

Sometimes during a processing, subjects sway or jerk their bodies. For example, one person who was processing fear of the
dark began to sway in a circular manner. The swaying became
faster and more vigorous. It lasted for about five minutes and
gradually subsided.

In another case, the subject's body rocked to and fro. Then
she jerked forward suddenly, such that her head was thrown
back and her facial expression showed that she felt some
pain. Later, her hips swayed very fast from side to side, as
in a dancing motion. This went on for about ten minutes. When
she was asked to be aware of the area that was swaying or of

tension in the body, the swaying diminished and eventually stopped.

Swaying or rocking is just the manifestation of energy imbalances in the body. When these are allowed to happen with awareness, they eventually subside and disappear.

CHAPTER TEN

Attaining a State of Relaxation

An important ability to develop in the self-transformation process is the *capacity to attain a state of functional relaxation when-*
ever there is no need for tension. It frees the consciousness energy
to be available for awareness instead of having it be sucked in
by psycho-physical tension.

Tension is a necessary part of daily life, and we move and
do physical actions by tensing the muscular system. The muscles also tense up when we have anxiety or anger or any other
negative emotion and the *ch'i* energy surges, readying the
psycho-physical system for action. During these states, the
psycho-physical system is not relaxed, that is, not at a zero level
of rest or relaxation.

When, however, the circumstantial pressure has eased and
there is no more observable anxiety or anger, many people still
do not return to a state of rest or relaxation. There is still tension
in one or more areas of their bodies. Usually the person is not
even aware of this continuing, chronic tension, which causes
tiredness and stress.

Functional Zero Level

We must learn how to achieve a *functional zero level* of tension on a moment-to-moment basis. It is called "functional" because it is not a *true* zero level of absolutely no tension. Some tension is required to maintain a practical level of alertness such as while working, talking, or walking.

This functional level depends upon the type of activity engaged in. For example, if we are engaged in a table tennis game, then the functional zero level will maintain a minimal state of tension so we can respond quickly to oncoming balls. The legs are bent, with spring-like flexibility and readiness. The arm holding the paddle is raised to the level of the chest, ready to move left or right. But we must not be *tenser* than is functionally necessary; otherwise, it will interfere with your responsiveness. A stiff arm and body—indicating excessive tension during a table tennis game—slows down response time to an oncoming ball. Such stiffness is not a functional zero level for a table tennis player. One becomes, in fact, less efficient or effective in the game.

The obstructive effect of unnecessary tension is found in many games and activities: in golf, an unwanted stiffness or tension interferes with the full swing of the club; in swimming, it enervates swimmers more quickly of their needed energy; in conversation, fiddling with keys and pencils affects the attention of the listener; in dancing, tensing the wrong muscles is guaranteed to lead to the loss of gracefulness. In each of these activities, however, a combination of tension and relaxation is needed for the optimal energy to produce the desired result, and the combinations are different for every activity.

The functional zero level of a table tennis player is different from the functional zero level of a person sitting on a chair reading a magazine. In the latter, the legs need not be bent and tensed to maximize agility. They can be completely stretched out and relaxed. The arms can be fully at rest, except for the muscles needed to hold the magazine. If the legs are tense while the person is reading a magazine, then that person is not in a functional zero level. That is *unnecessary* tension.

Self-awareness helps one achieve the optimal combination of tension and relaxation, which represents the functional zero level on a moment-to-moment basis. The table tennis player's forehead and shoulders should be relaxed. The grip on the paddle should be just sufficient and not too hard. The feet don't skip and jump and dance in a state of edgy anticipation. Any of these unnecessary movements or tensions will be noticed if one is aware, and they will naturally cease when they are noticed. When reading a magazine, you may notice that your legs are unnecessarily tense. Noticing it will allow the legs to return to a natural state of relaxation. These examples can be applied to any state of human activity.

The functional zero level is not merely a state of tenselessness. It is also the attainment of emotional calm in daily life. A calm state makes possible a sensitivity to your own emotions and to the emotions of others.

Virtual Zero Level

The *virtual zero level* of tension is different from the functional zero level of tension. It is the maximum level of tenselessness for a human being. This is achieved in meditation or in the death pose in Hatha Yoga. At this level, practically all voluntary muscles are in a state of rest. There is no surge of energy ready for any anticipated response. In meditation, this state of relaxation is evidenced by a very shallow level of breathing, almost imperceptible, indicative of the body's low need for oxygen and *ch'i*. It is evidence of a low level of biological, emotional, and mental activity in the person. Brain wave activity at this state would indicate either alpha, delta, or theta waves.

This level is called *virtual* because it is not necessarily an absolute level of tenselessness. The latter may not be possible, for it is a state that is of no use. Biological and psychological life needs activity. Even in death, many people go to their graves with their life's tensions intact.

Psychological Zero Level

The functional zero level of tension makes possible another state: the *psychological zero level*, a state of awareness in which thoughts are nonreactive and have no tendency to form opinions, likes, dislikes, and judgments. In this state, the mind is not busy with thoughts. Psychological zero level is not a useless or dysfunctional state. On the contrary, it is one that enables the inner or subtler states of consciousness to interact directly with reality. The intuitive function is active, and true impersonal action, not just personal reaction, becomes possible.

As the functional zero level makes possible a high degree of skill in human action, so the psychological zero level opens up the possibility of greater human understanding, resulting in superior assessment and response to a situation, particularly when coupled with self-mastery. The assessment of situations is on an intuitive level rather than a logical level. At the intuitive level, we are capable of seeing beyond appearances, for we are no longer absorbed or distracted by conditioned responses, whether emotional or mental. Thus, physical pain is no longer seen as disagreeable or something to be shunned. Rather, it is seen as a sensation that has a biological purpose and is psychologically neither likeable nor dislikeable. We may feel the sensation of "pain," but we do not experience psychological misery. Neither is there personal liking or disliking of people, which is a conditioned—hence superficial—response to people. Instead, there emerges a different quality of reality about people that is deep, authentic, and compassionate.

Of these three zero levels, the first one to explore is the functional zero level. Self-awareness processing is the most direct step to attaining this level on a continual basis. Self-awareness processing frees us from the energy congestions and push buttons that cause unnecessary tensions. Only when the functional zero level is attained on a regular basis can the other two levels be possible.

Four Approaches to Daily Self-Awareness

Here are four approaches to nurturing daily self-awareness. Endeavor to make them integral parts of daily behavior. The first effect of these habits is diminished chronic tension and stress. Ultimately, they bring about a quality of moment-to-moment mindfulness that has a transformative effect in one's life.

Abdominal Breathing

Make this your normal breathing, instead of the shallow chest breathing. Abdominal breathing tends to relax the whole body and calm the feelings. Try to consciously breath this way as often as you can. Eventually, it will become an unconscious habit.

Speaking from the Stomach

A tense person tends to have a high-pitched voice; a person in panic may even have a shrieking voice. On the other hand, a very relaxed person tends to have a round, sonorous voice. When we wake up from a very restful sleep, we have a low-pitched voice. Our state of tension is reflected in our voice quality. One tends to follow the other. One way of maintaining a low tension level, therefore, is by speaking from the stomach. This is done by producing sound from the diaphragm and abdomen without tensing the voice box.

To practice speaking from the stomach, try pronouncing words beginning with "h" but without the "h" sound: *hay, home, high, he, hip, him.* Be conscious of any holding effort in the throat area. Let the voice box just reverberate to the passage of the air. When you have gotten the skill, then practice it by regularly reading in this way.

Thinking from the Spine

Have you noticed that you can think from different parts of your head and body and that these modes of thinking are correlated with your level of tension?

There are three modes of thinking. The first is thinking from your forehead, the second is thinking from the back of your head, and the third is thinking from your spine. We often see people knitting their eyebrows in an expression of anxiety or worry or anger. Hence, they usually form permanent grooves between their eyebrows. If we do this deliberately, we notice that there is a corresponding tension in the head, particularly the forehead and scalp area. This is the first mode of thinking. People who constantly think this way will be more susceptible to headaches and early graying of their hair. Try it now. Knit your eyebrows while looking at something. Be aware of your scalp and the back of your neck. Do you notice the tension? If you do, stay with the tension so you remember how it feels. Then, in the state of awareness, allow the tension to subside, letting your head muscles relax.

While still aware of your head, look at the same object again, this time with awareness of any possible tension. Observe where you tend to be thinking *from*. Where is the center of your present consciousness? This leads us to the second mode of thinking: thinking from the back of your head. You may notice that, although the first mode seems focused on the forehead area, this second mode is somewhat diffused in the head. You may even notice that you are more conscious of the base of your skull at the back of your neck. And you will notice that you are more relaxed watching the object you chose.

Stay with this mode of thinking for two or three minutes. Become familiar with the difference between the first and the second mode. Notice whether the muscles of your scalp or forehead or eyebrows are tense. Feel any sensation at the sides of your head, temples, or other part of the head.

The third mode is thinking in which your awareness includes the spine. When you do this, notice that you are practically aware of the whole body, including the extremities. In this mode, you become aware of all the states of tension connected with thinking. Notice that there is minimal tension in this kind of looking and thinking. There is self-awareness. At the same time, you tend to experience a deeper perception and understanding of events, conversations, and situations.

Try to make this third mode of thinking your normal mode while you are walking, conversing with others, reading, watching TV, riding in a moving vehicle, observing the surroundings—in other words, while engaged in practically anything where you perceive or cognize something with your mind. Practice it as often as you remember until it becomes second nature.

Pausing before Acting

There is a fourth approach to nurturing daily awareness that will arise naturally from the practice of the previous three. This is to pause before acting. This pause is really a pause of awareness, not necessarily in terms of time. It may take just a fraction of a second or up to a few seconds.

As you are about to read the next words, take that pause of awareness. Be aware of your head, your body, your feelings, your thought-reactions, and your attitude at this moment. See whether your shoulders and arms are tense while you are holding this book. Be aware of the reason why you are continuing to read these lines.

Before you speak to someone, take the pause of awareness. Before you answer the phone, take that pause.

The Buddhist monk Thich Nhat Hanh offers a version of this pause with his "telephone meditation." He suggests that when the phone rings the first time, take a deep breath. On the second ring, have a smile on your face. On the third ring, pick up the phone.

These four tools must be consciously practiced as frequently as possible until they become part of your nature. If this is done with diligence, you will surely notice the change in your life in a few months' time.

The Nature of Emotional Pain

Books on psychology and physiological psychology tell us that emotions are accompanied by physical changes in the body such as decrease in salivation, increase in skin perspiration, and secretion of epinephrine or adrenaline. What they don't usually mention is the arousal of *ch'i*, which is discussed earlier in this book. The arousal of *ch'i* accompanied by physiological activity such as activation of adrenaline, increase of blood pressure, or tensing of muscles is what we call emotion, whether pleasant or unpleasant. It can be triggered by a cognition (seeing or remembering) or by a facial expression (frowning or smiling). When no energy flow is triggered, there is no emotion.

In this chapter, we look into the nature of emotional pain but not into the nature of all types of emotions. Joy as an emotion, for example, is not a problem and hence can be left as it is without any interference or processing, unless we have an incapacity to experience joy or a resistance to experiencing joy.

Why does the sight of a snake cause energy arousal, known as the emotion called fear, in one person but not in another? Young Susan has been told about poisonous snakes and their dangers. She now sees a snake. She presently believes (cognizes) that she is in mortal danger. Her whole body prepares to flee, triggering the release of adrenaline (and *ch'i*), and she runs to a safe place. Now safe, Susan directs her attention to, or is distracted by, other things, and she ignores the surge of energy that is still ongoing. Somebody converses with her about an entirely different topic, and her mind is distracted from the fear experience. The flow of the energy is stopped, thus freezing it somewhere in the system. This frozen energy stays there as a block or congestion until released. It may stay there for ten days, ten years, or a lifetime.

The next time Susan sees a snake, her biological system sends out the fight-or-flight energy or *ch'i* response, pushing or putting pressure on the frozen energy that is clogging her system. This triggers the trapped energy, which she feels as an unpleasant energy movement in her body. It might be a strong sensation, or it might be weak, depending on the quantity of frozen energy that is triggered. This energy that she feels is the fear. *The biological response of fight or flight that is accompanied by a rush of adrenaline or ch'i doesn't constitute fear itself. It is the triggering of this frozen energy that is felt as fear.* This triggered energy is felt as a hardening in the pit of the stomach, a sinking feeling, or a weakening flow of energy in the extremities. It may be felt as a tingling sensation or warmth. When strong enough, it causes numbness or even stiffness of the muscles.

When the body has no energy blocks or congestion during times of tension or crisis or danger, the natural energy flows and is felt as heightened alertness or preparedness, like a table tennis player's heightened state while playing, which is not fear.[1]

When we experience fear, it means that some prior unpleasant experience has accumulated a reservoir of energy in specific parts of the body that has not flowed out when it was aroused. This congestion of energy is stimulated by the cognition of the threat. *Emotional pain, therefore, is the distressful presence of this energy congestion that is triggered by a memory, a situation, or a stimulus.* When this congestion dissipates, the emotional pain disappears.

This understanding of the nature of emotional arousal is based on thousands of processing sessions with people whose fears or anger or resentment disappeared after the congested energy was allowed to flow or be released through processing. Such release normally occurs within thirty minutes, although in a minority of cases it takes much longer.

We now look into the nature of unpleasant emotions, and see how self-awareness processing resolves many emotional burdens very quickly.

Basic and Derivative Emotions

There are various kinds of unpleasant or painful emotions. Some examples are hurt, resentment, anger, irritation, rage, fury, wrath, worry, fear, guilt, envy, jealousy, sadness, depression, gloom, melancholy, loneliness, anxiety, panic, shame, embarrassment, exasperation, annoyance, anguish, distress, aversion, disgust, remorse, regret, and despair.

There are many types of unpleasant emotions, but there are only a few primary emotions. The other emotions are derivatives of these primary emotions. Knowing how to handle root emotions enables us to deal effectively with the secondary derivative emotions.

As far as we can presently determine, there are six primary negative emotions. They are fear, anger, hurt, aversion, dejection, and guilt. These primary emotions are not reducible into one another. This list is not meant to be final and does not include the positive emotions, such as joy, because we are presently only concerned with effective management of emotions that are obstructive to human growth and maturity.[2]

Fear

Fear is a biological reaction that has been embedded into our system for self-preservation. We share this reaction with animals. In human beings, however, the fear reaction develops into deeper levels of complexity and subtlety that engender a wide variety of derivative secondary emotions.

Research with infants shows that they have only two natural fears: fear of loud sounds and fear of falling. All other fears, including fear of snakes, the dark, strangers, heights, and people, are acquired. Fear is a major cause of human unhappiness and a serious obstacle to growth, so much so that the self-transformation process devotes special attention to it.

The following list describes the secondary derivative emotions of fear:

Worry is a mechanism of the psyche that prompts one to do something. The prompting energy is fear—usually fear of some consequence. Because it is fear, the person tends to avoid thinking about it. Thus, worry tends to perpetuate itself in a circular way—the fear causes non-action, and non-action causes worry. Chapter 17 is devoted to this important negative emotion and how to deal with it.

Anxiety is a fear whose object is nonspecific or vague, whereas worry is about something specific and identified. Anxiety is the result of repeated unprocessed fears that have accumulated in the subconscious. It is a vague feeling about an impending misfortune, but one that can't be dealt with because it is unspecified. To resolve anxiety, it must first be converted to specific worries, and then one can apply the guidelines on how to handle worry.

Panic is an overwhelming fear that makes one confused and unclear about what to do. This is the accumulated result of many fears, worries, and anxieties that haven't been resolved or handled well. It sometimes results in *panic attacks*, those inexplicable feelings that may not have an immediate cause.

A *phobia* is a fear reaction that is either out of proportion to the actual danger, such as jumping and shrieking at the sight of a rat or cockroach, or irrational, such as trembling when seeing the photo of a spider.

Trauma is a psychological wound that continues to cause distress. Strictly speaking, acquired fears are actually traumas in varying degrees of intensity. But a trauma becomes pathological when it causes periodic distress such as having nightmares, reacting intensely to anything that reminds one of the trauma, or severely disturbing one's daily life and work.

Envy is a complex emotion, being a mixture of a number of things: low self-esteem, resentment, and fear. We don't envy the successes or achievements of people we can identify with, that is, those we love and care for. Their achievements are vicariously ours, too. On the other hand, the achievements of people we can't identify with, particularly those we resent, are felt as threats to our own self-esteem.

Embarrassment involves a loss of face and being confused and perplexed at the same time. The embarrassment may not have been caused by anyone, as when one slips and falls down in front of people. Hence, there is no cause for anger toward anyone (except perhaps oneself). Embarrassment manifests as withdrawal and hiding and not wanting to face people. At its root is the fear of what people might think or say.

Shame is a similar feeling. It is fear of rejection, or a feeling of being rejected by others. At the root of it is an unhealthy self-esteem.

Fear engenders not only secondary or derivative emotions, but also certain psychological states or personality characteristics. These include the following:

Insecurity is a subtle and chronic psychological state of being unable to cope with perceived threats, whether physical, psychological, or social. It is rooted in fear and is somewhat different from the felt flow of emotions such as anxiety or panic. It is the outcome of the subconscious accumulation of fears. A person who experiences insecurity is hardly aware of the feelings connected with insecurity but nevertheless behaves according to these fears. When the various forms of fear are resolved through self-awareness processing, however, the sense of insecurity disappears.

Low self-esteem is a state that is characterized by poor self-regard, insecurity, and the desire to be loved and appreciated. It is no longer an emotion, but an attitude or psychological state. It is rooted in distressful experiences that have not been properly processed and have sunk deeply into the subconscious mind.

Anger

Anger has biological roots. It is manifested in the aroused state of the body that is ready to fight or attack. Physical and etheric *(ch'i)* energy is summoned from one's reserves and discharged into the system to respond to the emergency. Animals bare their teeth and arch their backs; their hair bristles, and they look fierce.

Among humans, anger has acquired a level of complexity and subtlety such that it is no longer a question of fighting with teeth and claws. Social norms have checked the outward expression of such an arousal, resulting in constant suppression and the building of another kind of congestion within the system.

Anger doesn't start as anger. It is preceded by irritation. But irritation in turn doesn't start with irritation. It is preceded by a subtle feeling of discomfort or displeasure that often goes unnoticed. And because the discomfort is unnoticed, it is unresolved and tends to build up into irritation or anger while the stimulus for the discomfort continues to be present.

When anger is unresolved and builds up, it becomes rage or fury. In that state, we are no longer in control. We have reached a state that psychologists call *mental incapacitation*, and our behavior will now be controlled by rage rather than by reason. There is a tendency toward violence, and if we hold a weapon, we can injure or kill another person we care for.

There are degrees of anger, but discomfort isn't one of them. We can feel a discomfort without being angry. The following list describes some of the derivatives of anger:

Frustration is the feeling of not being able to do something about an undesirable state. It is usually accompanied by irritation and anger and leads to aggression.

Irritation is a mild level of displeasure about a person or a situation and is accompanied by impatience or anger.

Rage is a violent and uncontrolled anger. It is the result of accumulated anger and is like the eruption of a volcano.

Wrath is strong anger accompanied by malevolence or sometimes by hatred. It is manifested as a feeling of righteous indignation.

Hurt

Feeling hurt is not usually one of the fundamental emotions listed by psychologists. But our observations in self-awareness processing indicate that it is an emotional reaction different from the others. It is not a form of fear; neither is it anger or frustration. Being hurt is a feeling in which self-worth or self-esteem seems to have been assaulted. It is a psychological reaction that differs from anger and fear, which are more closely rooted to biological origins. Feeling hurt may be analogous to the biological drive toward self-preservation and survival, except that in this case, it is the preservation of the psychological ego, the sense of selfhood.

The energy response to hurt is withdrawal, and its physical focal point is in the chest area. It is a sinking feeling, at times like a stabbing feeling in the chest, around the heart area.

When a husband or wife ignores the spouse or says or does something that seems to take the other person for granted, the spouse may not become angry, but hurt. When the hurt is not accompanied by anger, the person might just sulk or withdraw and feel the hurt alone. It is like being wounded, and the wound needs time to heal.

But being hurt is often accompanied by a feeling of being a victim of injustice; hence, it is at times accompanied by indignation and resentment.

Here are descriptions of some of the derivatives of feeling hurt:

Feeling insulted is a feeling of being degraded by others. The reaction is usually accompanied by anger.

Self-pity is self-indulgent lingering upon hurts and sorrows.

Depression can arise from self-pity, which may have arisen from a hurt.

Resentment is hurt mixed with irritation or anger. We may be angry with a certain child, but we don't necessarily resent the child unless we have been personally affected or hurt.

Hatred is an intense level of resentment. In this case, there is anger, not simply irritation.

Dejection

Dejection includes a group of emotions that are difficult to classify but characterized by lowness of spirit and diminution of psychological and physical energy. It can be caused by the loss of something or someone, loss of hope, or a separation from an object of attachment.

Here are descriptions of some derivatives of dejection:

Sadness is characterized by a low energy level, a lack of motivation and interest, and a loss of zest. It is more of a mood and may not be caused by a loss of anything.

Depression is a state of despondency accompanied by self-depreciation, low energy, and feelings of inadequacy. There are two kinds: the normal depression that is a temporary low point and dissipates over time, and the neurotic or psychotic depression that is deep, long-lasting, and is sometimes accompanied by suicidal tendencies.

Despair is a loss of hope. It is different from sadness but shares the same lowness of energy.

Grief, as a word, is used in many different senses. Often it is used to describe a bitter sense of loss of a loved one, which would fall under this class of emotion (dejection). But grief is also sometimes used to refer to bitter remorse, which would place it under the category of guilt (see below).

Aversion

Aversion is an intense inclination to avoid something. It is repugnance or revulsion, a strong dislike or distaste for something. Aversion is different from fear, although they bear similar features. For example, aversion to caterpillars may involve the unpleasant feeling that one is crawling on the arm. The unpleasant feeling usually evolves into a fear of caterpillars. Aversion to slimy things or to dung, however, may not evolve into a fear.

Disgust for certain foods can be experienced as a nauseated or queasy feeling.

Guilt

Guilt is a feeling that results from a perceived violation of a particular moral code or principle.

Remorse is a more intense feeling of distress due to guilt.

Emotions and Energy Movements

Each of the six basic emotions has corresponding locations in terms of the movement and congestion of the *ch'i* energy in the physico-etheric system.

Fear of an impending event is often felt as a movement or congestion of energy at the pit of the stomach or solar plexus.

It may feel like there is a hard ball or butterflies in the stomach. When actually faced with a threat (height, snake, etc.), the reaction is often felt in the limbs, with such feelings as trembling, weakening, or freezing.

Anger is almost always felt in the head, although it may be followed by pain or heaviness in other parts of the body, such as the back, when the flow of the aggressive energy gets arrested in those areas.

Hurt is felt in the chest, usually on the left side, about two inches to the left of the breastbone. It can feel like a stabbing pain or a hard, congealed ball. A heaviness on the chest may be felt that makes breathing more difficult.

Dejection or *sadness* involves a weakened feeling, a lack of psychic and physical energy. Depression, which is the extreme form of dejection, is conducive to thoughts of suicide because there is no energy—hence no motivation—to resist, struggle, or fight the threat.

Aversion, when not associated with fear, is felt as nausea or other forms of unpleasant physical sensations, such as standing hairs at the thought of caterpillars crawling on the skin.

Guilt is felt in the center of the chest, at the lower part of the breastbone. It is also felt as heaviness.

In all these reactions, there is an energy disharmony or congestion or withdrawal. Restoring the natural flow of energy in the affected areas and throughout the system effectively removes the distress. Although this statement may appear to be a simplistic approach to such serious disorders as traumas and phobias or depression, you can verify it for yourself through experimentation and investigation before brushing it aside. Years of experience in the Self-Transformation Seminar and counseling sessions by seminar facilitators have repeatedly affirmed the effectiveness of this approach in helping relieve individuals of their emotional pains.

Emotions and Self-Awareness

In the discussion in the previous section, we find that within each group, emotions may differ from one another only in terms of degrees but not in kind. For example, there are many degrees of fear, ranging from a simple discomfort toward some object to a full phobia of the same object. Self-awareness prevents the escalation of a distressful emotion without suppression. It also enables an emotion to naturally ebb into a state of equilibrium or equanimity.

Let's take the emotion of anger as an example (see figure 11.1).

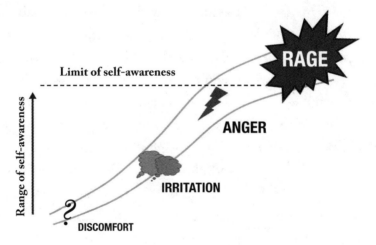

FIGURE 11.1. **How Anger Develops**. Anger starts from discomfort and irritation and, if unattended to, may develop into uncontrolled rage.

Anger is a medium-level emotion that has grown out of irritation and discomfort. As previously explained, anger does not pop out immediately as anger, except when a conditioned push button has been developed. It is always preceded by irritation. Irritation, in turn, is always preceded by discomfort or tension. When we are not aware of a discomfort, it may grow into irritation. When we are not aware of an irritation, it may grow into anger. And when we are not aware of the anger, it may become rage or fury. In this last stage, people become "mentally incapacitated." They are no longer reasonable; they lose control of themselves, thus the oft-heard statement that "anger is temporary insanity." It is the pent-up energy bursting out from the system. The energy demands to be released through violent ways, such as throwing things, hitting someone, punching the wall, or shouting. When it is suppressed, we feel trembling in the body, and the blood pressure is likely to shoot up.

In the diagram, there is a horizontal line labeled "Limit of self-awareness." This means it is possible to be self-aware when we feel discomfort, irritation, or even anger. But when we cross the line into rage or fury, then there is no self-awareness, and such an enraged individual becomes a dangerous person not only to others, but also to himself or herself. The surging energy is so strong that it will either be externally released, resulting in the injury of other people (or to oneself such as when one punches a concrete wall), or internally suppressed, which can cause a heart attack, a stroke, or apoplexy.

When there is self-awareness, the energy is allowed to flow naturally and thus does not build up into a more intense form. Discomfort is likely to be resolved at its level, without the necessity of developing irritation. Neither does irritation grow to become anger. Anger does not turn into rage.

Self-awareness, then, can effectively deal with discomfort, irritation, and even anger, either in preventing their escalation or in allowing the safe release of the rising energy.

Expression versus Release

Sometimes, we read of books that advocate the expression of an emotion such as anger in order to cure oneself of the distressful feeling. Many workshops use this approach to release anger. I once read that in one Japanese factory, the company provided a room in which a pillow was tied to a post. The pillow had a drawing of a face on it. When workers were angry or frustrated at their supervisors, they could go into this room and punch the pillow as a way of venting their anger.

Does this method solve the problem of frustration or anger? I think not. It may temporarily release dangerous pent-up energy, but it doesn't solve the frustration or anger within.

Expressions of hostility don't necessarily diminish the hostility itself. In fact, research shows that expression can intensify hostility. In one study, one hundred laid-off engineers were interviewed. Some of them were asked questions that allowed them to vent their hostility. When the entire group was later given a questionnaire regarding their attitude toward the company, it was found that those who vented their anger showed more hostility than those who hadn't.[3]

Self-awareness processing is a nonviolent approach to releasing stored energy. The release of the energy resolves the emotional distress or pain permanently. In itself it does not solve the external conflict that caused the internal distress, but the release of the congested energy removes the push-button reactions that tend to blind the person to objective reality and prevent the person from resolving the problem effectively. In fact, as we will see later in the chapter titled "Effective Relationships," self-awareness is an essential foundation stone for effectiveness in dealing with people. Without it, techniques about listening or communicating do not work very well.

Measuring Distress

A convenient measuring tool for self-awareness processing is the subjective unit of distress (SUD) developed by S. Wolpe. It is the range from zero to ten in which a subject rates the strength of distress, with zero being no distress or pain and ten being extreme distress or pain.

This measuring tool is useful for two reasons. First, it tells the facilitator that the subject is still uncomfortable. If the subject says "Three," then the facilitator asks, "Where do you feel this three? Scan your body and see where you feel the discomfort." Second, it helps the subject know whether he or she has had an improvement in the internal feeling of distress. Sometimes subjects take the process for granted and don't realize that they have achieved a better state of relaxation.

I had been chatting informally with about six staff members of an institution prior to the start of a session, and I felt that they were more or less relaxed, judging from the way they were interacting with me. It therefore surprised me when one of them said that she was 9 on a scale of 0 to 10 and two others were 7. I realized that my external evaluation was very different from a subject's internal assessment of distress. True enough, it was the staff member at a level 9 who broke down later because of a minor discussion about an issue with another staff member. What I failed to glean from personal interaction, the SUD was able to reveal.

How to Use SUD

When a subject is already in distress at the beginning of a self-awareness processing session, the facilitator should ask, "On a scale of zero to ten, where zero is complete relaxation and ten is extreme distress, how would you rate yourself right now?" When the subject is really distressed, expect an answer at a minimum level of five.

If the subject is not distressed at the beginning, the facilitator should then ask for the SUD only after the subject has recalled a person who has angered or upset him or her.

After the processing, when the subject has already attained a state of relaxation, the facilitator should ask again for the SUD; generally, the answer will be zero to two. If it is a two, the subject still feels slight discomfort. The facilitator should then ask where it is being felt, and if needed, continue to process it.

The facilitator should ask for the SUD several times during the processing session, whenever the facilitator feels the information will be useful.

Examples of Processing Sessions

To better understand the procedure for scanning and emotional processing, I have included two example sessions below. Please take note that the words used during the processing are carefully chosen to avoid suggestions, except in two aspects: first, to remind the person to breathe deeply, and second, to ask where the person feels the sensations during the in-breath and outbreath cycles. Other than these exceptions, the facilitator should be asking merely "what" questions.

Scanning

Most scanning sessions involve minor heaviness or pains, such as shoulder pain. In some cases, however, a session may touch on emotional issues. The actual case below is an example of a scanning session that involved emotional issues. There was no discussion about any personal problems prior to the session. Neither did the subject discuss the matter afterward, except for what is mentioned at the end of the example. The time between pauses is approximate, as this was recorded from memory afterward, rather than transcribed from a recording. The italicized notes in parentheses are comments on the process.

FACILITATOR: Sit comfortably, with your palms on your lap and feet on the floor. Breathe in deeply from your abdomen at least five times with your eyes closed. (*Pause for sixty seconds.*) Now, as you continue breathing from your abdomen, scan your body and check whether you feel any tension or discomfort. Do you feel anything on the top of your head and the back of your head? (*Pause for ten to twenty seconds.*)

SUBJECT: (*Shakes her head slowly.*) No.

F: How about your forehead and eyes? (*Pause for ten seconds.*)

(*Subject raises her hand and touches the middle of her chest, the lower part of the breast bone, or sternum.*)

F: You feel something in your chest?

(*Subject slowly nods her head affirmatively.*)

F: What do you feel in your chest?

S: Pain . . .

F: How large is it?

S: Like a ball . . .

F: Is it hard or soft?

S: Hard.

F: As you breathe in deeply, feel this pain in your chest, and as you breathe out, feel the sides of your chest, including your arms and hands. (*Pause for a few seconds.*) Do not fight the pain. Just experience it fully. Do not try to change it. Just be aware of it fully. (*Pause.*)

The energy tends to flow toward the arms; hence this instruction.

(*Subject knits her eyebrows slightly and presses her lips tight.*)

F: If your body feels like crying, it's all right to cry.

This assurance is helpful, because many people are embarrassed to cry.

(*Tears began to flow from subject's eyes. Her lips began to loosen after about thirty seconds.*)

F: What do you feel now?

S: (*Slowly nods her head.*) It feels better now, but my head is painful.

F: Where in the head?

S: Here. (*She touches the left portion of the back of her head, around the area where the parietal and occipital bones meet.*)

F: As you breathe in, feel the pain in that area. As you breathe out, feel the back of your neck, including your shoulders and back. (*Pause for one minute.*)

S: The pain has eased. I feel again a pain in my chest. (*She puts all her fingers on the left side of the chest, two inches from the middle of the breastbone.*)

F: Is it a large area? Or a small area?

S: Small, like something piercing.

F: As you breathe in, feel this pain. As you breathe out, feel the left side of your chest, including your arms and hands.

S: (*After about one minute.*) My throat . . . as if something is blocking it . . .

F: What part of your throat?

(*Subject touches the area between her Adam's apple and collarbone.*)

F: As you breathe in, feel the constriction in this area. As you breathe out, feel the surrounding areas of your throat, including your mouth area. (*Pause.*)

Again, this instruction follows direction of subject's energy flow.

S: This is numb. (*She touches her jaw region*).

F: Feel the numbness as you breathe out. (*Pause.*)

F: (*After one minute.*) What do you feel now?

S: (*Nodding.*) The numbness is less . . . the block in my throat is still there but smaller . . .

F: Continue the deep breathing, feel your throat as you breathe in and feel your mouth as you breathe out. (*Pause.*)

F: (*After a minute.*) What do you feel now?

S: I feel all right now. My throat feels all right.

F: No more block?

S: No more.

F: How about your mouth?

S: No more. It is not numb anymore.

F: How about your chest?

S: (*After about twenty seconds.*) No more. It's all right.

F: No more heaviness?

S: No more.

F: How about your head?

S: It's all right. No pain.

F: Can you now check your entire body to see if there is still any part that is uncomfortable or tense? (*Pause.*)

S: (*After about thirty seconds.*) Yes, I feel relaxed.

F: Completely relaxed?

S: Yes.

F: Do you feel tired?

S: Yes.

It is important to check visually whether the subject is truly relaxed. Observe whether the body is loose, rested, or still tight.

F: It is normal to feel tired after a processing. You may now open your eyes.

After the session, the only thing that the subject mentioned was that she felt like shouting when she was feeling the blockage in the throat. She didn't elaborate on the cause or circumstance.

In this case, although the objective was merely to scan and release congestions in the body, the subject was actually already processing an emotional issue, even though she wasn't aware of the connection with any memory or experience.

Processing an Emotional Issue

The following is a shortened account of a much longer processing session that took about an hour and a quarter. It was induced by a surge of emotion the subject felt while doing the scanning. She felt bitterness and resentment about a person she thought she had forgiven a long time ago, because the other person involved had died.

FACILITATOR: Go into deep abdominal breathing for five times. (*Pause until five breathing cycles are completed; then silence for about a minute.*)

As much as possible, start from a state of relaxation.

F: Now I would like to ask you to think of a person or an incident that has hurt you or angered you or upset you. Breathe deeply as you do so, and tell me what you feel in your body. (*Pause and wait.*)

(*The subject begins to sob heavily, and tears flow down her cheeks. She seems to be holding her breath after every in-breath.*)

The facilitator keeps silent while the subject is crying.

F: (*After about a minute.*) What do you feel now?

SUBJECT: (*Touches her throat and chest.*) My chest is heavy, and there is a small object in my throat, like a ball.

F: As you breathe in, feel the heaviness in your chest and the ball in your throat. As you breathe out, feel the surrounding areas including your arms and hands, as well as your mouth and jaws. (*After a one-minute pause.*) What do you feel now?

S: I feel heaviness in my chest. (*Touches her chest.*)

F: Feel the heaviness in your chest as you breathe in. (*After about a two-minute pause.*) What do you feel now?

S: There is no more heaviness in my chest, but there is a pain at the back of my right shoulder. I feel also tightness in my thighs.

F: Feel the pain in your right shoulder as you breathe in, and then when you breathe out, feel your legs and feet.

(*Subject goes through the process in silence on her own for a few minutes.*)

F: What do you feel now?

S: It's gone now.

F: Your shoulder?

S: There's no pain anymore.

F: How about your legs?

S: It's all right now.

F: Can you check whether there is still any tension anywhere?

S: (*After about thirty seconds.*) I feel relaxed now.

F: Now I would like to ask you to think of the same person or incident again and tell me what you feel.

This is the second cycle on the same issue.

S: (*Touches her temples.*) There is pain here . . .

F: As you breathe in, feel the pain in your temples. As you breathe out, feel the back of your neck, shoulders, and back.

(*Subject goes through the processing for a few minutes again in silence.*)

S: It's gone now. There is no pain anymore.

F: Can you check again whether there is still any tension elsewhere?

S: I feel relaxed now.

F: Now I would like to ask you to think of the same person again and tell me what you feel.

This is the third cycle on the same issue.

S: (*After about two breathing cycles.*) My head feels heavy, and there is tightness in my throat.

F: Then feel the heaviness in your head as you breathe in, as well as the tightness in your throat, and then as you breathe out, feel your body and arms as well as your mouth.

(*Subject goes through the processing for a few minutes again.*)

S: It's OK now; the heaviness and the pressure are gone.

F: Can you check again whether there is still any discomfort in any part of your body?

S: (*After a pause.*) I feel relaxed.

F: Think of the same person and incident again and tell me what you feel.

This is the fourth cycle on the same issue.

S: (*After a few moments, she slowly shakes her head.*) I don't feel anything anymore.

F: Check if you're completely relaxed.

S: Yes, I'm completely relaxed.

F: Do you feel tired? Would you like to continue?

S: Yes, I can continue.

F: Now I would like to ask you to think about another incident connected with this person and tell me what you feel.

This is the first cycle for the second incident.

S: (*After a pause.*) I feel heaviness here. (*She points to the heart area on the left side of the breastbone.*)

F: Then feel it as you breathe in and feel the side of your chest and arms as you breathe out.

(*Subject is silent for a few minutes.*)

F: What do you feel now?

S: I feel all right now on the chest, but I feel heaviness in my head.

F: Go ahead and feel the heaviness in your head as you did before, as you breathe in and out.

S: (*After some minutes.*) I feel all right now; there is no more heaviness.

F: Can you think again of the same incident and tell me what you feel?

This is the second cycle for the second incident.

S: (*After being silent for a few moments.*) I feel heaviness again in my head.

F: Then go ahead and feel it as you breathe in and out.

S: (*After a few minutes.*) It's gone now. There is no heaviness anymore.

F: Can you think of the incident again?

This is the third cycle for the second incident.

S: (*After some moments, she slowly nods.*) No, I don't feel anything anymore. I feel relaxed.

F: Can you think of another incident connected with this same person?

This is the third incident to be processed.

(*The subject's face changes, and she again sobs bitterly. The facilitator doesn't ask anything for a minute or so while she is crying.*)

F: Breathe in and out deeply again and feel fully whatever sensation you may be having in your body.

(*Subject does the breathing and is silent for some time.*)

F: What do you feel now?

S: I feel all right now. There is no heaviness anymore in my chest.

F: Can you think again of this third incident and tell me what you feel?

This is the second cycle for the third incident.

S: (*After a few moments of silence.*) I feel all right. I don't feel anything about it now. I feel relaxed.

F: I would like to ask you to open your
eyes now and to think of the person in
these incidents and tell me what you
feel about him.

S: (*After some moments of silence.*) I am
at peace with him now. I thought
that I had already overcome this
pain, because I read a book about
forgiveness and I already forgave him.
But I now realize that I still had this
deep pain within me.

Emotional issues can be shallow or very deep. The range and
variety can be extremely wide. Experience is the best teacher
when it comes to understanding how to handle different situations. In time, we learn how to address most circumstances at
the moment they occur. Soon these skills become almost second nature to us.

Dealing with Fear

Fear is basically a biological reaction to a threat. Its symptoms are tension, weakness, hollowness in the stomach, and trembling, among others. When a threat doesn't produce these symptoms, the person is either indifferent to the threat or may be concerned but not afraid.

The line that separates simple *concern* from *fear* may be difficult to draw or may differ from person to person. Concern is essentially a *compassionate impulse* that seeks to alleviate or prevent pain and suffering in other people. It comes from the upper triangle, the inner self. It is not self-centered. Fear, on the other hand, is a *self-protective reaction* that is accompanied by *personal distress.* Concern doesn't bring about personal unhappiness, but fear does.

Another factor that distinguishes fear from concern is the extent to which such a reaction (such as tension) would distort judgment or reasonableness of response to the threat. Fear usually distorts the perception of a situation, whereas concern tends to allow for being objective.

People know there is some risk in riding in an airplane, but they fly anyway, and throughout the flight, some people feel relaxed, have fun, and go to sleep easily. Even when air pockets shake the whole plane, they still feel calm and may even joke about it. They are, of course, concerned about their safety, but there is no fear.

Contrast this with people who know the same risk about airplanes but feel frozen the whole time they are on a plane. Days before a flight, they may have butterflies in the stomach or tension in the shoulders just thinking about the coming flight. They are concerned about their safety, just like the other people, but in addition, there is a fear reaction.

It is this fear reaction that must be dealt with. Such fear distorts perception of external reality, affects soundness of judgment, causes unhappiness, and reinforces the self-protectiveness of the ego, which tends to obstruct spiritual awakening.

The Intensity of Fear

How we deal with fear depends on two factors: the intensity of the fear and the strength of the inner will.

Mild Fear

When the fear is negligible or mild, we may be able to easily overcome such an obstacle, unless the will is so weak that no effort is made to overcome it. In that case, we need to strengthen the will.

Intense Fear

In cases where the fear is intense, we must work on the neutralization of the automatic fear reaction. Such intense reaction is a veritable obstacle to effective and wise action. The reaction of fear is basically irrational, and it can easily dominate our behavioral tendencies. For this level of fear, self-awareness processing is perhaps the most effective way of making the fear disappear completely.

The Irrationality of Fear

Fears produce reactions that defy reason. Estela, for example, was so afraid of spiders that she couldn't even look at the picture of a spider. Whenever the letter *S* was mentioned, she reacted in fear because she remembered that the word *spider* starts with an *S*. Reason tells us that it is obvious that a photograph isn't harmful, not to mention the letter *S*. But the physico-emotional system is conditioned otherwise.

Jenny is an accomplished professional who has won awards for her work. She has fear of snakes. When she was young, she could not write the letter *S* because it reminded her of a snake. When she had to write a word that contains *S*, she would first write all the other letters and ask her sister to write the letter *S*. When her family went out together for dinner and her father ordered noodles, she would not eat them because they reminded her of snakes. For fear that her father might get offended if she did not eat, she would allow him to put the noodles on her plate, but would immediately transfer the noodles to her sister's plate when her father was not looking. Some readers may find these stories funny, but to these people, such fears are serious.

Fears can affect major decisions in life, such as the choice of careers (one who fears blood will never choose to become a doctor), or turn away from life-changing opportunities (such as turning down a scholarship abroad because of a fear of riding in airplanes). Fear can make us dangerously ineffective, like a lady who froze during a fire instead of running out of the building or being able to help others.

It is essential that we must rid ourselves of all forms of fear. The state of fearlessness is different from courage. Courage is needed only when we have fear. When there is no fear, there is no need for courage. People who have no fear are not necessarily reckless individuals. They can still be highly prudent and careful and aware of the risks involved. One may not be afraid of heights, but that does not mean that the person will stand carelessly on the edge of a tall building.

During seminars, I am often asked this question: "But how about the fear of the Lord? Should we also remove such fear? Does not the Bible say that 'the fear of the Lord is the beginning of wisdom'?" The original word for fear in Hebrew is *yare*, which can mean fear, but it also means awe or reverence. The King James translation uses the word *fear*, which probably reflects the actual attitude of the ancient Hebrews toward Jehovah, who is described as a wrathful and jealous god.

But a moment's reflection will show not only that fear is not an indicator of wisdom, but that such an attitude is psychologically unwholesome and contrary to the later Christian teaching about love of God as the first commandment. (Matt. 22:37–8)

It is extremely hard, if not impossible, to fear and love someone or something at the same time. Aristotle observed this more than two thousand years ago when he wrote: "No one loves the man whom he fears." We always avoid what we are afraid of. If I am afraid of spiders, I avoid them. If I am afraid of my father, I avoid him. If I am afraid of the Lord, will I go toward him? I will not.

There is a gulf of difference between fear and reverence. When we revere or respect certain people, we don't fear them. We are careful not to displease them, but we don't avoid them. Hence, the more appropriate idea behind the verse quoted earlier should have been, "*reverence* for the Lord is the beginning of wisdom."

But fear does not stop with avoidance. Shakespeare wrote: "In time we hate that which we often fear" (*Antony and Cleopatra*). People who fear cockroaches have the automatic tendency to kill them. When we fear Christians or Muslims or Jews, we eventually hate them. This is the probable root of many kinds of social violence that we observe in our midst.

Kinds of Fear

Fears can be classified as physical fears, social fears, and fear of the unknown.

Physical Fears

Physical fears are the fears of identifiable objects or environments, such as snakes, cockroaches, lightning, dead people, coffins, heights, deep water, and so on. They usually originate from unpleasant or traumatic experiences in the past. The built-up, congested energy has not flowed normally, and hence it elicits an unpleasant physiological reaction whenever we see or remember the object of fear.

Social Fears

Social fears are connected with people. As I mentioned earlier, the greatest fear of human beings is the fear of rejection, which includes being humiliated and criticized and being the object of what people might talk about. The fear of public speaking belongs to this category. So does the fear of failure. Note that the fear of failure is a social fear—a fear of what people will say if one doesn't pass a board exam or doesn't reach a sales target or is unsuccessful in business. Individuals have been known to commit suicide when they face humiliation. To them, death is a less painful alternative to disgrace.

Fear of people is an unpleasant reaction that may have originated from past distressful feelings when the individual was reprimanded, criticized, humiliated, or laughed at. At its root, then, are frozen energies that person continues to carry. These energies are triggered when the possibility of being humiliated again is subconsciously sensed and the fear reaction arises. The way to deal with fear of people, therefore, is to process the congealed energy connected with the fear, and allow it to flow.

Fear of the Unknown

The fear of the unknown includes the fear of death, of ghosts, and of hell. These fears are more complex, because they are a mixture of beliefs, frozen energies, and unpreparedness. We can include in this category the fear of loss of things or people.

Let's take the fear of death as an example. The fear of death can be due to the fear of the pain of death or fear of annihilation or fear of going to hell or fear of separation from loved ones or a combination of these. It is somewhat more complex than the fear of objects or people. Such fear can be due to several different reasons, described here.

Ignorance. People fear that death means the end of everything. The best way to conquer this fear is to find out what we know about death from research. That there is life after death is almost certainly a fact. There is so much evidence for it that we only need to look into the documented research on near-death experiences, reincarnation research, and psychical research to be convinced of it.

Another aspect of this fear is the mistaken belief that death is painful. From the research of thanatologists (those who study death), we have discovered that the process of dying is not painful. In fact, serenity is frequently observed among those who undergo the death transition. If ever there is pain or suffering, it doesn't come from dying itself but from whatever disease the person is suffering from. Studies in near-death experiences, in fact, show that death releases the person from the suffering.

Unpreparedness. Another source of fear of death is unpreparedness. What will happen if one were to unexpectedly meet an accident and die? Would he or she leave a mountain of mess to the family? Do they know about the person's indebtedness, bank accounts, and other important things? People often don't think about these things because they dread the thought of death. But the less they prepare for them, the more they will be afraid of death. Hence, it is advisable to arrange affairs and documents now, so that if anything happens, instructions have been left with somebody who will be able to efficiently attend to matters that need attention.

Incomplete Relationships. A third source of fear of the

unknown, particularly the fear of death, is what we may call incomplete relationships. Some people are afraid to part with people when relationships are unfulfilled or incomplete. When they haven't expressed their care and affection for their loved ones, it is hard for them to imagine parting from the loved ones. When people haven't given enough time and attention to their aging parents, they dread the thought that the parents may die. If this is the case, then they must give time and care to those they love. That love must be expressed in some way, and not necessarily verbally. It can be a regular visit. It can be a long and pleasant conversation. It can be through thoughtful gifts or letters.

Trauma or Phobia. Some people have a trauma or phobia of death, which is a conditioned reaction to the thought of death because of some unpleasant experience in the past. This can be resolved with self-awareness processing.

Processing Fear

Most fears are due to the triggering of congested energy within the psycho-physiological system, resulting in an unpleasant feeling that we want to avoid. Allowing this energy to flow to normalcy will allow the fear reaction to disappear. Processing fears, therefore, is essentially the same as processing emotions. However, the procedure differs a little. Let's take processing the fear of public speaking as an example.

Subjects who fear speaking in public are first asked if they are willing to overcome the fear through the self-awareness process. They are told that at any stage they are free to discontinue, and that nothing will be done without their prior permission.

If they agree, then they are first asked to imagine themselves being asked to possibly speak to an audience the following day. Those who have a phobia of public speaking will already react physiologically to this *imagined* thought that they will *possibly* have to speak. It can be an increased heart rate, tension in the arms and legs, hardness in the solar plexus, or weakness in the knees.

When such reactions are reported by the person, then the facilitator asks the subject to breathe in deeply and be aware of the discomfort or heaviness or numbness. These will eventually subside, and the person will go into a state of relaxation.

After being certain that the person has become relaxed and calm, the facilitator asks the subject to imagine facing a small group. The subject is asked if he or she feels anything in the body. Specifically ask about the body parts that had previously had sensations during the first processing. If the subject still has some sensations, then the facilitator asks the subject to go through the self-awareness processing again, until the whole body goes back into full relaxation.

The facilitator then asks the subject to imagine facing a larger audience. It is likely that discomfort will again be felt. The facilitator goes through the same processing procedures until the subject attains relaxation. Note that the imagined scenarios during the processing go through graduated stages, from slightly threatening to more threatening scenarios.

When the subject feels relaxed imagining facing an audience, the facilitator asks the person to stand in front of a room (any empty room) and imagine being on the stage facing a large audience. If the subject feels relaxed doing this, then the person is encouraged to try standing in front of an actual group and saying something about himself or herself.

When these steps are done properly, the subject will be free of the phobia of public speaking. (This doesn't mean that the person will no longer be nervous when speaking to a group. Nervousness is different from a phobia.)

The procedure is similar for all kinds of fears that involve involuntary distressful reaction to an object or imagined thing. The following are more examples:

Fear of the Dark

The facilitator asks the subject to imagine being in the dark, and then the facilitator helps the person process. The facilitator then accompanies the subject to a room and asks permission to turn off the light, then again processes any discomfort. After relaxation, the facilitator asks for permission to leave, tells the subject to self-process if there is any discomfort, and to come out once full relaxation is achieved.

Fear of Heights

First, the facilitator asks the subject to imagine being in a tall building and to process any discomfort. The facilitator then accompanies the subject to a tall *but safe* location where the subject can look down from the heights to the ground. The facilitator then guides the subject to process the reaction until relaxation is achieved. Then they try other locations.

The above procedures can be adapted for other kinds of fears. A basic principle is this: *when the psycho-physiological system is in a relaxed state when we are faced with what we fear (i.e., the object, image, or memory), there is no fear.* It is the distressful bodily reaction that constitutes the fear experience. The conceptual understanding of the presence of a threat or danger does not in itself constitute a fear.

The Deeper Layers of the Fear Experience

The fear of objects or people is the most tangible or external manifestation of fear, but there are more subtle types of fear that are less noticeable yet operate in the same way as external fears. These subtle types come in the form of hesitation, avoidance, and dislike. Detecting these fears requires a comprehensive and deep level of awareness.

For example, when someone is coming toward me, I may consciously or unconsciously avoid that person by going to the restroom. I am not experiencing any palpable fear, and yet I am avoiding that person, which is a symptom of fear.

When someone disagrees with my belief or opinion, I may start to dislike that person or even react with righteous indignation. Such reactions may be a sign that I perceive the person as a threat.

Awareness of these subtle reactions can lead to freedom from such automatic subconscious patterns. It involves a processing on a far subtler level of experiencing. It needs the depth of the meditative mind—one that is conscious of the different layers of thought-reactions.

Case Studies

Experience is the best teacher when it comes to self-awareness processing. As facilitators process more and more people, they become more sensitive to what is happening when a person undergoes internal experiences. Such sensitivity guides the facilitator in asking helpful questions that make the process more effective.

The following short summaries of actual cases illustrate different kinds of personality problems or internal conflicts that are helped by self-awareness processing. Where necessary, the circumstances have been modified to respect the privacy of the people involved.

Stress and Neurosis

Willy was a successful professional who in the past few years had developed phobias. He could no longer go out without a companion. He used to drive by himself for long out-of-town trips lasting for days, but now he feared driving by himself. He had to take heart pills daily, because he had heart palpitations and high blood pressure. He had begun to take sleeping pills because he couldn't sleep easily. He had consulted doctors who told him that they couldn't detect anything wrong with his heart or cholesterol level.

Then, he went through the self-awareness processing three times, with intervals of one week after each session. At the first round, which lasted for less than an hour, he felt pressure in his chest and found that he felt like sobbing. He was told by the facilitator that it was all right to cry, and he began to sob uncontrollably while his body heaved in a jerky manner. He felt pain on his head, which was released through the extremities. His arms and hands felt numb. After the energy flowed, he felt calm and said that he felt tired.

When he came back the next week, he said that he no longer needed sleeping pills to sleep, and he could now go out alone. When he underwent the self-awareness processing the second time, much less energy was released.

After the third session, he happily related his experience to anyone who would listen to what was happening to him. He had stopped all heart pills because he no longer had high blood pressure. He could drive by himself and no longer needed to be accompanied. The fears that had been troubling him had totally disappeared. He sleeps so well that he now goes to bed very early. He has also started a vigorous exercise regimen.

Family Relationships

Elsa was desperate about her domestic problems, which involved constant quarreling with her husband and extreme resentment toward her aunt, who lived with them.

While she was undergoing self-awareness processing, she

was asked to think of her aunt. She started to cry and felt pressure on her head and the left side of her whole body. She went through two cycles of the self-awareness exercise.

After four days, she came again and said that there had been a drastic change in her feelings at home. She could now talk with her aunt, and she no longer reacted angrily at her husband. She looked very excited and happy and shared her experiences with members of a regular group that she was attending.

Chronic Pain and Stress

Edwina had chronic back and shoulder pain every day. She was sometimes unable to get up from her bed and had to ask someone to lift her up so she could stand. Her doctor thought it was due to her scoliosis. At work, she was highly stressed by the pressure of her responsibilities. Her high tension level had begun to affect her effectiveness at work.

She underwent self-awareness processing with deep abdominal breathing and began with a simple scanning of her body. She felt pains on her head and back of her neck. The most painful part was a small ball the size of her thumb on her right shoulder, connecting to the lower back skull and the back. When she felt it the first time, her face grimaced with pain. She had to be assured that it was all right to go through the pain, because she was trying to resist it. After one cycle of self-awareness processing, the pain subsided. On the second cycle, the ball was less painful. On later cycles, the ball didn't appear there anymore, but the pressure spread to the other shoulder.

After going through more than eight cycles of processing

for specific worries, anger, and resentment, she entered into a state of relaxation in which she felt sleepy and tired. While she was resting and allowing herself to go to sleep, she said that she was feeling strong pressure in the temple area pressing inward to the center of her forehead. Then the energy went to the left breast area with intense heat. The energy went diagonally to the inside of the breast and then was released through the nipple. This happened very quickly.

When she met the facilitator again after about one week, she reported that the back pain she had experienced every morning was now gone, and she could easily get up from bed. She now uses the self-awareness process to deal with her every-day tensions and is much less irritable than before.

Fear

Martha was a prominent professional who was respected for her executive ability and judgment. She had a number of pho-bias, one of which was fear of the dark. She couldn't sleep with the lights off. She had to prepare herself to turn off the lights in the living room because the switch was at the main door, and her bedroom was down the hall. She had to run the moment she switched the light off.

She agreed to process her fear. We went to the living room of a friend's house, and with four of us accompanying her, we told her that we would switch off the light. She was previously told about the process, and when she became frightened, she was asked to describe what she was feeling in her body. She described the tightness in her stomach and the trembling of her arms and hands. As she breathed from the abdomen and felt this tightness and trembling, the physical sensation began to subside. Gradually, she became totally relaxed. We then asked permission for one of us to leave the room. She agreed. When the person stood up to leave, she began to feel the tensions again, but this time with a lesser intensity. She went through the self-awareness process again until her whole body became calm and relaxed. One by one, we asked permission from her for one of us to leave. By the time the last one was leaving, she felt comfortable with her reaction pattern, and she agreed to stay in the dark living room alone. She was told that she could leave the room any time she wished to, but we suggested that she leave the room only when she had become fully relaxed. She did stay, and when she left the room, her fear of the dark had disappeared.

Memory and Image Clarity

A painful memory or a resentment is often accompanied by a sharp and clear image of the person or event being recalled. We commonly observe that after the self-awareness process, when the resentment disappears, the image becomes blurred and hard to recall or recreate.

Alma was a dynamic, highly intelligent executive. She was a high achiever, but one thing weighed down her life. It was a bitter resentment toward her father, who was still living with her. When she started the self-awareness process, the images of painful incidents connected with her father were very clear and vivid. She began to have headaches and hard balls at the pit of her stomach, which she processed for about thirty minutes. After the numbing and tingling sensations subsided, she tried to recall the incidents connected with her father again, and she said that they weren't clear anymore. Her resentment toward her father also disappeared.

Energy Blocks Interconnected

The energies of one emotional block may be connected with the energies of an emotional memory of a different nature. During one seminar, Lynn wanted to overcome her fear of public speaking. Since this involved fear and we would be having a special session for that, it was agreed that we would deal with other forms of emotional distress first and deal with the fear the next day.

Lynn went through the process of self-awareness through breathing, and the first thing that came to her was the memory of how she was maltreated by an aunt when she was a small child. She started sobbing and having pressures and heaviness in various parts of the body. With the facilitator, she worked on this for about an hour, until her resentment toward her aunt dissipated. After the session, she felt pity and understanding toward her aunt, rather than anger and hatred.

The next day, at the start of the session on conquering public speaking, Lynn suddenly said that she was no longer afraid to speak in public. She felt that the fear left with the energies that flowed when she was processing her resentment toward her aunt the previous evening.

Trauma

Martha attended the Self-Transformation Seminar, and when everyone was asked to do deep abdominal breathing, she said that she could not do it. She felt a thick, heavy thing on her entire chest that she described as a "concrete block." We guided her on how to proceed despite this block, and while doing the processing, she sobbed and trembled. Her extremities became numb. After more than forty minutes, she entered into a state of relaxation, and the chest pressure completely disappeared. When asked what she felt, she smiled and said that she felt light, and she felt like dancing.

We learned that four years previously, two of her family members had died in accidents within a span of several months. She had a breakdown, and for two years she was under psychiatric care. Her cheerfulness faded, and she could not think of the two loved ones without crying or at times getting hysteric. Her work was affected. After the processing, she could think of the two family members without feeling distressed.

On the next day of the seminar, I discussed death and our fear of it for about thirty minutes. After the session, Martha spoke to me and said she was amazed that she could listen to my talk on death calmly. Prior to that, she hadn't been able to listen to talks about death without breaking down and crying. She was convinced that she was already free of the trauma of the two accidents.

Pain

George was a priest who was at first reluctant to participate in the scanning and self-awareness processing. He just wanted to observe and learn. When he was told that he would lose nothing by trying it, he agreed to try the process.

During the scanning, a facilitator sat with him as a partner, and he went through awareness of different parts of the body. After the session, we were surprised when he volunteered to share in front of everyone what he experienced.

George said that for thirteen years he had been having a chronic pain in his back, just below the right shoulder. He had consulted doctors and had his back massaged many times, but the pain remained. During the scanning session, he followed the direction about just being aware of the pain while doing abdominal breathing. He was surprised when the pain disappeared. He turned and twisted his neck and body to check whether it was still there, and he could no longer feel it. During the three days of the seminar, the pain did not come back. We have not seen George again since he lives in another country, but I suspect that the pain is permanently gone unless he accumulates new stresses.

The range of distresses that can be normalized by self-awareness processing appears to be so wide that we constantly discover new areas of application as the years go by. The normalization of conditioned push buttons through the natural release of energy blockage seems so basic to the relief of psychological distress that we now see it as an important key to wholesome psychological health.

Effective Relationships

I have been discussing self-awareness, which is an effective approach to attaining self-mastery and resolving inner pains and conflicts. But there is a major source of emotional distress that must be attended to if one wishes to attain lasting inner peace. This concerns relationships with people.

It can be said that the main source of human unhappiness is problems in relationships with others. When we lose money or a car, we may feel upset for a day or a week, but we soon forget about it and get on with our lives. But when we have problematic relationships—especially with people who are close to us—the distress may last for ten years or fifty years. It can affect work, relationships with other people, and sometimes the very meaning of our lives.

Ellen had been having difficulties with her husband, Fred. She suspected that Fred was having an affair with another woman, but Fred denied it. This suspicion deeply hurt and angered Ellen, but the more she talked to Fred about it, the angrier Fred got. The issue was like a wedge between them that was separating them further and further apart. Ellen was stressed, and it was taking its toll on her office work. Her attention had been called to a number of recurring mistakes she had made on her job. At home, her children didn't understand her irritability on small things, such as being short one fork on the dining table. She had a hard time getting to sleep and had started taking pills. In her distress, she occasionally thought of ending her life. Fred noticeably distanced himself from Ellen. He didn't even want to go out with her and the children on weekends anymore.

Ellen's life is not unique. In most aspects, she represents millions of people whose lives have lost their meaning because of problems in relationship.

Because this problem is so important and because it robs humanity of happiness, the process of self-transformation must deal with this source of distress and conflict. What must be learned and developed are a set of inner qualities and a set of outer skills.

Three factors contribute to wholesome and effective relationships: self-awareness, active listening, and harmonious assertiveness. The self-awareness process has been discussed in previous chapters. This section deals with two other factors, active listening and harmonious assertiveness.

Relationship is a two-way process in communication. A person tries to convey thoughts and feelings to another person, and conversely that individual tries to do the same thing toward the first person. When such communications are received and conveyed objectively, calmly, sensitively, and kindly, then the chances are very high that the relationship will be harmonious and positive. But when such communications are accompanied by underlying resentment, fear, anger, or hurt, then they will be blocked, distorted, misunderstood, or aggressively conveyed. These feelings arise from unresolved push buttons within the psyche.

It is important to realize that self-awareness is an essential prerequisite to effective listening and communication. When push buttons are still strong, there is an automatic and subconscious tendency to block messages because they are perceived as painful or unpleasant. Such push buttons also interfere with attempts to communicate with other people. One becomes either timid or aggressive when there is unprocessed fear or anger. When they have been processed and the congestions are allowed to flow, then listening can become genuine and effective; expressions of one's thoughts and feelings will be sensitive and constructive and will help resolve conflicts rather than add to them.

Active Listening

Active listening is one of the most important ingredients in an effective and fulfilling relationship. It even has a healing effect. It is the simplest and most direct way of resolving difficulties between people.

During the Self-Transformation Seminar, we ask participants to divide themselves into groups of three. Each person has the chance to be a sharer, listener, and observer. The sharers are asked to talk with the listeners about a significant or memorable experience in their lives. The observers observe what is happening between the two. Was the listener really listening? Was the sharer encouraged or discouraged to speak?

After the session, the participants share with one another the behaviors they noted that contributed to effective listening and those that obstructed listening. The facilitator writes the behaviors down on the board under four columns. Figure 15.1 shows a typical list of behaviors that participants give. As participants read through each column, important implications become obvious to them, and probably to you, too. Add your observations on effective and ineffective listening and their effects on you as the sharer.

Note that the helpful listening behaviors can elicit joy, relief, affirmation, and happiness in the person speaking. The unhelpful behaviors, on the other hand, can produce resentment, unhappiness, low self-esteem, and discouragement.

HELPFUL LISTENING BEHAVIOR	EFFECT ON SHARER	UNHELPFUL LISTENING BEHAVIOR	EFFECT ON SHARER
Holds eye-to-eye contact	Has greater self-confidence	Looks elsewhere	Loses interest in sharing
Asks clarifying questions	Feels: respected	Shows no facial reaction	Feels: hurt
Nods	encouraged important	Looks at watch	unimportant insulted
Has appropriate facial expression	good happy	Has no eye contact	offended unappreciated
Leans forward	inspired motivated	Fidgets	angry worthless
Affirms what is said	relieved loved	Plays with pencil	like turning away
Is not distracted by other things	closer to listener	Interrupts	
		Tells own story	
		Gives advice	
		Does something else	

FIGURE 15.1. Behaviors Influencing Effective Listening. This chart shows helpful and unhelpful listener behaviors and sharer reactions to such behaviors.

Ask yourself which kind of listening is happening in your own home right now. If it is similar to those listed in the first column, then your family members are probably happy people. If it is similar to those listed in the third column, then they are probably unhappy people, particularly in their relationships with one another. Take note that this is happening every day, 365 days a year.

Genuine listening has a magic that is almost unbelievable. Tony was a very unhappy and troubled young man when he approached me after a meeting. He wanted to leave his house because he couldn't stand his father anymore. The father was always scolding him, and Tony would turn his back and walk away whenever his father started his harangue. Tony cried as he shared his situation, because it was difficult for him to decide to leave.

Tony agreed to first process his anger and resentment. He did the self-awareness processing, and his whole body was trembling as the energy of the push buttons was being released. His resentment toward his father dissipated after about thirty minutes. He felt exhausted and rested a while. Then I told him that I had a suggestion. He nodded and said he was willing to do whatever I suggested. I told him that the next time his father started reprimanding him, he should stop whatever he is doing, go up to his father, look at him, and then really listen to what his father says. He was, of course, astonished that I should even suggest this to him, since listening to his father was the last thing he wanted to do. But I assured him that it was worth trying for at least two weeks. I made this suggestion because he had already processed his anger toward his father, and because he had processed, he was actually more willing to try the suggestion.

We met two weeks later. He greeted me with a big smile and laughed when he told me what happened. When his father had started to scold him again, Tony stopped what he was doing, approached his father, looked at him, and truly listened to his father instead of going out the door and slamming it. (Note that he could now do this genuinely because he no longer had resentful push buttons within him.) Within five days, his father changed. He stopped preaching, and the rest of the family began to feel differently toward him. Over the next few months, he melted and became closer to his children. Tony decided that he would stay at home and not leave. His father was no longer a problem in his life. Tony could now converse and joke with his father. The family members developed a much closer bond among themselves.

The most powerful way of dealing with angry people is to listen to them—not only to their words, but also to their feelings and frustration. Listening doesn't mean agreeing with them; it means understanding them. It means caring for them. (It is a bit different if the other person is in a state of rage, for that person is no longer sane. But it still works in many cases of rage, provided there is no violent danger involved.)

Listening has a healing effect. It can heal the deep wounds of the soul. Dr. William McGrath wrote, "Ninety percent of all mental illness that comes before me could have been prevented, or cured, by ordinary kindness." That kindness starts, and can even end, with simple, genuine listening. Dr. Elton Mayo wrote, "One friend, one person who is truly understanding, who takes the trouble to listen to us as we consider our problem, can change our whole outlook on the world."

Children feel loved when parents listen to them. Unconsciously, their self-worth is reaffirmed every time someone truly listens. Many families take children for granted. Elders ignore them when they are asking for, or inquiring about, something. Parents who are doing paperwork or household chores or reading a newspaper don't even bother to look at their children when the children talk to them. Every time this happens, a child's feeling that he or she is unimportant is reinforced.

I strongly suggest that parents develop the habit of interrupting what they are doing whenever a child approaches them for something, unless the task is something that really can't be interrupted (such as when talking to someone on the phone). This kind of interaction creates self-esteem and self-confidence in the child. Even if the parents don't say "I love you," the child feels loved.

When the task can't be interrupted, then tell the child that you will just finish your present work and you will talk after, say, ten minutes. After ten minutes, remember your promise. The child will most probably be waiting.

For older children and teenagers, listening to parents works magic, too. Children who really listen to their parents find that their parents tend not to be so hotheaded or prone to reprimanding. One of the best ways to deal with a fuming father or mother is to listen to him or her.

A family whose members can listen to one another is most probably a happy family. Not that they are free of problems, misfortunes, or conflicts, but the way they deal with these problems and conflicts doesn't engender interpersonal resentment and anger.

Harmonious Assertiveness

Along with self-awareness and active listening, the third element for a wholesome relationship is effective communication, which requires harmonious assertiveness. There are three ways of responding to people when we encounter any kind of conflict: we can be *timid*, *aggressive*, or *assertive*.

Timidity avoids conflict but leaves the timid person hurt or burdened. Aggressiveness doesn't avoid conflict, but when people are aggressive, they use words or approaches that tend to intensify or worsen the conflict.

Assertiveness, on the other hand, helps a person face a conflict without worsening the situation. It is accomplished by being careful not to use accusatory words that would make the other person feel defensive. We describe our own reactions rather than the supposed motives of the other person. Judgment about the other person's character is avoided, unless the situation calls for it, such as when a supervisor is evaluating a subordinate. (There is a fourth way—mature silence—which is a transcendent way of dealing with conflict under certain situations. I do not take it up in this book, because a person who responds in this manner has already solved the problem of conflicts in life, whether intrapersonal or interpersonal.)

Figure 15.2 describes some salient characteristics of the three approaches.

It will be helpful if you, by yourself or with a group, try to imagine different social situations that have potential conflicts, and then determine how people will handle the situations if they are timid, aggressive, or assertive.

TIMID	AGGRESSIVE	ASSERTIVE
You are afraid.	You lose control.	You are calm and self-aware.
You don't speak, or you lie or are improperly apologetic.	You accuse or judge the other person, using statements that start with "You are . . ."	You state your reaction, feeling, or opinion without accusing or judging others, using statements that start with "I feel . . ."
You suppress your feelings.	You vent out your anger; you manipulate the other person's feelings.	You express your feelings sincerely and honestly.
You suppress your own right.	You violate the rights of others.	You exercise your own right.
You evade the conflict but don't resolve it.	You create more problems and conflicts.	You resolve the conflict more effectively.

FIGURE 15.2. Approaches to Dealing with Conflict. This chart illustrates the three modes of dealing with conflicts and the characteristics of each mode.

Here is an example of a scenario: A female assistant in an office is the subject of a false rumor that she is having an affair with her boss. She knows who started the rumor. How will she handle it?

- Timid: She may just suppress the feeling of hurt, or she may just rationalize that it is untrue and not do anything about it. She begins to avoid certain people and no longer feels at home or happy in her work.

- Aggressive: She goes straight to the person, say, a female officemate, who started the rumor and starts quarreling with that person in the presence of others, accusing her of being an idle gossiper who has her own shady affairs.

- Assertive: She approaches the person and asks for a private time to discuss something. During the meeting, she calmly shares what she heard. "I was told that you had mentioned that I am having an affair with my boss because I am often seen having dinner with him. I don't know whether you really said it or not; that's why I wanted to talk with you. I just want to let you and others know that I have no personal relationship at all with my manager. He often asks me to join him at dinner to discuss things we were unable to finish during the afternoon. I will be glad to ask him to explain to all of you about our work relationship so that there will be no misperception about things."

Notice that in the "assertive" example, the assistant is not angry or accusatory in her words. She qualifies her information by saying that she does not know whether what she heard was true or not. When words are couched this way, the other party does not feel accused or judged and will not feel defensive in his or her own response.

Here are a few other scenarios:

A husband makes a derogatory joke about his wife's cooking during a party at their friend's house. The wife feels hurt and embarrassed. On the way home, she is silent and uncommunicative. When they arrive home, the husband says, "You are very silent. Are you bothered by something?" How would the wife respond if she were timid? Aggressive? Assertive?

A person is riding a public transport (bus or taxi) and he is disturbed by the loud rock music inside the vehicle. How does he behave if he is timid? If he is aggressive? Assertive?

A group of friends are celebrating a birthday when another friend happens to drop by. The group now asks the newly arrived friend to drink alcohol with them "for the sake of the birthday celebrant." But he doesn't drink alcohol and doesn't want to. How does he handle the situation if he's timid, aggressive, or assertive?

In each scenario, it is important that when the assertive situation is depicted, the assertive person doesn't resort to lies or false excuses, but rather, tells the truth. (Usually, lying is another form of timidity.) How can someone be truthful without being offensive? For example, in the case of the birthday celebration, the person must not say that a doctor told him not to drink. In the scenario, assume that he believes that drinking alcohol is harmful and he doesn't want to indulge in it. How does he convey this without offending his friends?

Lack of assertiveness leads to lying, even in the simplest of circumstances. When someone asks, "How do you like my new hairstyle?" what do you say when your honest opinion is that it looks horrible?

In developing the capacity for assertive communication, note that an important element in assertiveness is to be able to state a truth without triggering a defensive reaction on the part of the other person. Such a defensive reaction is elicited when we judge others, or when we are attacking or criticizing or condemning them. An assertive statement focuses on the event or action rather than the person, and describes one's own feelings or opinions about it. We therefore must choose our language, taking note that what is customary may often be aggressive (saying, "No, you're wrong," instead of stating your own alternative opinion) or insincere (saying, "No, I don't mind it. It's all right," when actually it is not).

Assertiveness is the product of two things: character and the acquisition of a skill. It is a character that is calm, kind, just, and self-aware. The skill is the capacity to choose words that are truthful but not unnecessarily hurtful or offensive. It takes practice to acquire this language skill. We must therefore constantly be aware of opportunities to be truthful and assertive.

Aside from the words we use, two other elements can contribute to the difference between aggressiveness and assertiveness: body language and tone of voice. When we approach another person with arms akimbo (fists on the sides of the waist), the impression that the other person gets is that we are already angry and aggressive even before we speak. When we speak with a loud or commanding tone of voice, the recipient may feel offended and threatened and become defensive.

Assertiveness skills include a familiarity with what is offensive or not offensive in a culture. Following are some examples:

- The phrase "you people" is offensive in some cultures or groups (such as in the Philippines) but not in others.

- A loud voice can be inoffensive in some cultures but threatening in others. In one South Asian country, I have observed workers sitting beside each other and talking loudly as if arguing, but they were actually just discussing in a normal manner.

- Looking at a person while talking to him or her can convey sincerity in one culture (as in Western countries) but can be disrespectful in another (as in parts of South Asia, particularly between young females and elder males).

- Calling another person by curving the forefinger upward is insulting in some cultures but not in others.

These are examples of cultural factors that can make the difference between an aggressive and an assertive approach.

Soliciting feedback from friends is a helpful way to understand whether one's behavior is aggressive or not. This can also be done in a growth group in which the members meet regularly to learn about facets of living that can accelerate self-transformation.

It is important for people to learn the skill of assertive communication while still young. Poor habits of communication are somewhat difficult to change after they have been deeply ingrained. Schools must teach good communication skills in primary grades so young children learn how to deal with conflicts effectively.

CHAPTER SIXTEEN

Love and Caring

We often speak of love, and yet we rarely see its manifestation in daily life. Lovers, husbands and wives, parents and children—they often say they love each other, and yet much of their behavior doesn't reflect this affirmation.

What is love? How is it distinguished from attraction, infatuation, desire, or dependence? Is romantic love genuine love? Is jealousy a sign of love? Is physically punishing a child a sign of love?

Modern culture has popularized certain meanings of the word *love*. These can often be gleaned from modern songs:

"I love you—because I need you."

"I'm lost in love; I can't live without you."

"Be mine tonight."

"What you did and where you're coming from, I don't care, as long as you love me, baby."

It is obvious that what we call romantic love is often characterized by the need or desire of the one who "loves." If I say, "I love you because I need you," what happens when I no longer need you? Do I cease to love you? If I say, "I love you because you're beautiful," what happens if you are no longer beautiful?

This kind of love is dependent on conditions. I give you love if you give me something else. If you don't, then I don't love you. This obviously isn't love. It is a business transaction.

The Nature of Genuine Love

What characterizes a loving or caring attitude or relationship? When people are asked to list what they think are the qualities of genuine love, they usually include qualities such as the following: respectful, thoughtful, willing to sacrifice, kind, open, considerate, understanding, selfless, patient, giving, generous, serving, helpful, sharing, and forgiving.

Note that all these words have one thing in common: they entail genuine concern and considerateness toward the other person, rather than preoccupation with one's own needs. Hence, we may say that the essence of love is a *concern for the welfare of another.*

Geoffrey Hodson, the eminent theosophical author, once spoke of one important key to happiness in marriage, and said that couples who practice this key will be guaranteed happiness in their married life. The key is, *always think of the welfare of your partner, and never of yourself.* When observing couples we know, we find this to be profoundly true. The happiest couples are those who are not generally preoccupied with trying to satisfy their self-centered needs, whether physical or psychological. In other words, their lives are relatively free from the imprisonment of psychological push buttons created in the past. Instead, they feel and exhibit a natural concern for the loved one.

Relating it now to our understanding of the dual nature of human beings, we find that love is essentially an expression of our higher nature, or higher triangle, rather than the lower. The lower triangle, representing a creature of needs and desires, is basically concerned with the satisfaction of these needs. It is oriented toward getting, rather than giving. Any act of giving from this level ("I love you . . .") is rooted in some kind of satisfaction that one derives from the other person (" . . . because you make me happy.")

Expressions of Love and Caring

Human beings respond positively and wholesomely to the love of other people. But such love must be *behaviorally expressed.* It cannot just remain as an intention or a wish. Many parents feel surprised and hurt when they hear that their children have said their parents do not love them. They feel hurt because they have been working so hard for their family, only to hear that their children feel unloved. These parents have failed to distinguish between intention and behavior. People are not clairvoyants or seers who can discern the innermost feelings of other people. They can only feel what is expressed or manifested in behavior, such as a kind word, a smile, a touch, a hug, a praise, a phone call, or a gift.

Behaviorally, love and caring are manifested through very simple acts that arise from the spontaneous appreciation and concern of others. Two such acts can make people feel loved even if we don't use verbal declarations of love (which in some cultures are difficult to express):

Listening
Listening is the most basic act of caring. Not listening is the surest sign of self-absorption, that is, egocentricity.

Genuine listening, as discussed in a previous section, means that we are ready to understand another person unconditionally. This doesn't mean that we should always agree with what is said. To understand doesn't mean to agree. They are very different things. In the process of understanding, there is no resistance from within. It is the conditioned reactions for or against what is heard that can obstruct true understanding of another person.

Behaviorally, this can manifest in simple situations. For example, when a child approaches you to speak to you about something, you pause whatever you are doing and face the child, preferably on the child's level (meaning you lower yourself so your face is at the same level as the child's face). Give him or her your complete attention, understand the meaning of the child's words and feelings, and afterward, respond appropriately, whether it is giving a simple acknowledgment, showing appreciation, making a decision, or turning down a request. (See below on firmness.)

When you talk to your spouse, look at him or her. Except perhaps for inconsequential or trifling exchanges of information like "Where's the newspaper?" every conversation is an opportunity for the expression of your appreciation or caring of your spouse. This is particularly true when your spouse is expressing some problems or difficulties or concerns. To listen genuinely to someone is one of the deepest affirmations of a loved one's importance.

When you talk to an elderly person, don't pretend to listen just to humor or console the person. Genuinely listen. When we extend this capacity to truly listen to anyone we meet, we begin to have a taste of what unconditional love really is.

Making Quality Time

In expressing care for the people around us, it is helpful to understand what the phrase *quality time* means. Quality time doesn't mean just spending an hour or a day with a person, as if it were an investment in time to show the person that we care. Quality time means that we are enjoying the time with the person. It means we appreciate the person.

When you go to the beach with your family, do you lie on the beach all day reading a novel? If you do, then it means your relaxation is more important than your companions. You went to the beach for your rest, rather than to enjoy things with them. But, you may say, what if I really need a rest? Isn't that what a vacation is for?

Then it means that you lack the time for them. Even the time that you are supposed to enjoy with them, you need for yourself. There is possibly a lack of balance in your life. It means stress has accumulated. Your family time is used for the purpose of unwinding. When will you have time for the people you "love"? Why, at times, are your dearest ones given the lowest priority?

In tiny bits of time at home, do you converse with your family or do something with them that you all enjoy doing? The positivity and enjoyment of the activity together is the essence of quality time.

Five Languages of Love

An insightful book about ways of expressing love to others is Dr. Gary Chapman's *Five Languages of Love*. In his practice as a family counselor, Dr. Chapman found that people express and perceive love in five different ways:

- Words of affirmation

- Quality time

- Physical touch

- Acts of service

- Receiving gifts

Most people have one or two primary love languages. If your daughter's language is quality time, and you express your love by showering her with gifts, she may feel that you don't love her, even though you do. This is because she doesn't understand the language of gift giving. It is helpful, therefore, to be sensitive to the primary love language of those close to you. Note that most people respond well to the first two, words of affirmation and quality time.

Sensitivity to the Needs and Feelings of Others

When we are habitually engrossed in our own needs and desires, we are usually blind to the needs and feelings of others. When we have processed our own needs and push buttons lodged in the lower triangle, we find that it isn't difficult to be sensitive to the needs of others.

Selflessness

To be genuinely concerned about the welfare of another means that we must not be absorbed with ourselves. Such absorption includes feelings of impatience, anger, and defensiveness, or being occupied with thoughts about work, worries, and other preoccupations. To attain this quality of non-egocentricity, we must process the internal, unresolved baggage and attain a higher degree of effectiveness and integration in the affairs of our lives.

Firmness or Assertiveness in Love

People often ask, "If we're too selfless, shall we not be easily abused by others?" One said, "Certainly if somebody slaps me on the right cheek, I won't give him my left cheek. I'll slap him back!"

A common misconception is that the loving person is a weakling or a pushover, a doormat for people to step on. This is because people understand love as a personality relationship, that is, belonging to the lower triangle or the outer self.

Consider Mahatma Gandhi—few are as loving and as selfless as he was. Was he a pushover? Not even the entire British Empire could budge him if he didn't want to move.

Love has no fear. It doesn't try to please in order to gain

the affection of the loved one. It has the wisdom that romantic feelings are often blind to. It can see the faults and weaknesses of the beloved and can say no to the beloved if what is asked for is not to that person's benefit. Let's look at two examples of assertiveness in love.

A mother who truly loves her child will not pamper the child or give in to every whim and caprice the child has. Love has firmness as much as it has clarity and kindness. A mother who can't say no to her child is a mother who has fear—she is afraid to lose the affection of her child. Thus, she is demonstrating a need rather than love.

A wife who loves her husband will choose to not cooperate in a matter that will, in the long run, contribute to the husband's unhappiness or will engender conflict between the two of them. But such a decision must emerge from the clarity of the wisdom of love and not from the fears, prejudice, or narrowness of the wife herself. Thus, love is wisely assertive.

Love and Attachment

A special aspect of love, one that is frequently questioned, is attachment. When we are fond of a person, there is often a feeling of attachment toward that person. We miss the person when he or she is away. We grieve when we lose the beloved. In other words, we have grown attached.

Is attachment a necessary part of love? Or is it possible to love without attachment? Let's look into it. When I am attached to something, what is happening? I feel comfortable when the object of love is present and feel deprived when that person is away. I feel a need for the presence of the other, and hence attachment is really an expression of my need. It is still the call of the self-centered lower self and is distinct from love. In fact, it may be said that, to the extent that there is self-centered attachment, to that extent is the love tainted with egoistic aspirations. But to be nonattached doesn't mean that there is no genuine appreciation of the loved one.

Appreciation

Appreciation is different from attachment. We can look at a sunset with wonder and awe without attachment. When the sun sets and darkness engulfs the sky, we don't yearn for the return of that scenery. Can we look at a painting or a movie in a similar way? How about a relationship? Can we fully appreciate the presence of a person while he or she is around and not feel miserable when the person is absent?

Incomplete Relationship

Here we face the issue about the incompleteness of relationship with other people. When an interaction and an experience of a person is incomplete, then there will be a desire to be with the person again, a yearning for the person. We tend to miss the individual. This is the manifestation of attachment.

When, on the other hand, an experience of a relationship is complete, there is no yearning for the person's presence when he or she is not around. There is no feeling of misery because of the absence of the other.

At any given moment, every individual we encounter has a certain significance to us. He or she may be a friend, a spouse, a son or daughter, or a coworker. This is really the essence of our appreciation of the person. When the other is in front of us, this appreciation manifests as an inclination to express something to or do something for or with that person. *This inclination is due to a psycho-physical energy that spontaneously arises because of an appreciation of the person.* The full experiencing of this feeling, this inclination, or this attitude, and the appropriate handling of it, give completeness to the interaction. After the interaction, there is no remnant yearning or desire for repetition of the experience or the presence afterward.

Suppose I visit my mother, who lives in another place. If I care for her, there will be certain things I will feel inclined to say or do while I am with her. They can be small things, like helping her clean or cook, or just having an hour of conversation with her. If, throughout the hour, I am able to fully experience my appreciation of her both within myself (such as feeling warmth toward her) and in terms of my behavior (helping her in her household chores), then the interaction is complete for that particular instance. I won't leave her house feeling sad or guilty or unhappy.

But if, during the one hour with her, I am not aware of my deeper feelings for her (that is, the feelings are there but I am just not consciously aware of them), then my actions and my conversations may not reflect this deeper attitude. In fact, I may behave in a contrary nature, such as reprimanding or criticizing her for not taking her medicine regularly or for not returning calls (which is how many people express their "concern"). At the end of the hour, I will leave my mother's house with a subconscious feeling of unfulfillment, even a feeling of righteous anger because "she doesn't listen to advice" or "she's very hard-headed." When my interactions with her are repeatedly of this nature, then I will be afraid to lose her—a feeling of being unprepared for the final parting. There is an accumulated feeling within, a psycho-physical energy that is not able to flow freely or completely, that causes this feeling of fear of losing. This is the cause of attachment.

Self-awareness enables us to be in touch with the attitude or feeling of appreciation and to act appropriately in accordance with its spontaneous inclinations. It is the factor that enables us to complete an interaction with a person from each moment to the next, from one meeting to the next, leaving no remnants within us that later result in attachment.

Unconditional Love

Can love really be unconditional—given without any expectation for oneself? If so, is that possible in practical life? Are we still human beings when we love without any expectation from the other?

There are two kinds of expectations between people: *relationship expectations,* or those expectations arising from an agreed or assumed relationship, and *egocentric expectations,* or those arising from the personal needs and desires of a person.

If I apply for a job and am accepted, I establish a relationship with the company, my superior, and my coworkers. This multifaceted relationship creates interpersonal expectations. I am expected to report at a certain time and do certain tasks that I have accepted. These are relationship expectations.

If I get married to a person, I am in effect pledging to certain explicit and implicit duties as a husband and a father. In a monogamous society, I am expected to not have a second wife or a similar relationship with others while I am a married person. By entering into marriage, I am agreeing to such promises, thus creating relationship expectations. In other words, there are duties that have been set and accepted. Such expectations are proper and do not arise from the self-centered needs of the individual.

Egocentric expectations are different. They are rooted in the psychological needs or desires of the person and may or may not have anything to do with the relationship expectations. When I expect my wife to remember my birthday, or that she should be responsive when I am in the mood for romance, then it is my egocentric expectations that are operating. There is nothing in the marriage arrangement that says the husband or wife should always be in the same mood as the spouse or that one should never forget the other's birthday.

Relationship expectations may differ from culture to culture, whether family culture, ethnic culture, or national culture. Egocentric expectations depend upon the upbringing and conditioning of the individual. Relationship expectations are more impersonal; that is, they can be taken as "duties," whereas egocentric expectations are personal.

Unconditional love can have relationship expectations but not egocentric expectations. Relationship expectations are due to perceived duties of the other party arising out of the relationship agreed upon. But because there are no egocentric expectations, we don't feel personally hurt or slighted for the omissions of the spouse or of other people. Thus, anger doesn't arise, even if some problems are perceived.

The keys to unconditional love are two: (1) the awakening

of the higher spiritual consciousness, which is compassionate and caring, and (2) the elimination of push buttons, or conditioned reaction patterns that engender hurts and frustrations.

When we deeply explore the nature of appreciation, compassion, caring, and loving, we begin to discover that what is called love is a kind of radiation from the inner being. It is like the sun that shines indiscriminately on all, or like the blossom that gives out its perfume to all, not even minding whether or not there are passersby. Love is essentially nonselective, but when filtered through our personalities, we feel preferences and favoritisms.

Love is essentially transcendent and not personal. It is the natural emanation of that spiritual nature within us that feels our nonseparateness with others. We feel for others; we feel with others. Their interests are spontaneously felt as our interests.

Feedbacking

Here is an exercise that can be done by any two people who are acquainted with one another sufficiently enough to be able to give substantive feedback to each other—such as husband and wife, brothers and sisters, friends, or coworkers. It is an activity that can deepen a relationship between two people and engender greater authenticity in the relationship. It also helps develop nonattachment through the process of listening to praise and criticism without push-button reactions.

This is a very powerful exercise, and it is assumed that the two people doing the activity have learned self-awareness processing, listening, and assertiveness.

While facing each other in a sitting position, each partner takes turns in giving three positive feedbacks. Each partner can request the other to give a negative or constructive feedback, which should be inserted between the second and third positive feedback. When no request for negative feedback is made, then no such feedback should be given.

Both partners must first go into self-scanning for a few minutes to ensure that they are relaxed and self-aware. After ensuring that they are in a relaxed state, they decide who will first be the giver of feedback and who will be the receiver. The receiver of the feedback says that he or she is ready to receive feedback. The giver should also be in a fully relaxed state. When there is nervousness or tension felt, then the giver should process these discomforts first before giving any feedback.

The giver of the feedback thinks of something that he or she admires in the other person. Then it is expressed in words truthfully, sincerely, and without exaggeration.

- The receiver, after hearing the positive feedback, checks to see if there is any automatic reaction to the feedback. If so, the reaction should be processed. It might be embarrassment, tension, tears, or any number of reactions. No explanation or justification or denial should be given by the receiver. The reaction should just be experienced and processed. During this stage, both the giver and receiver should be silent. (Note: The receiver should not assume that he or she has no reaction, then quickly ask for the next feedback. The receiver should be silent for at least one full minute, go into deep breathing, and see whether there is any discomfort, uneasiness, or tension in the any part of the body as a result of the feedback received.)

- When the receiver has finished processing the reaction and has reached a state of calmness and relaxation, then the giver should be told, "I'm ready for the next feedback."

- The giver gives the second feedback. The same procedure as above is followed.

- If the receiver requested negative feedback, then it should be given after the second positive feedback, using the same procedure. If no request was made, then go to the third and last positive feedback.

- Switch roles. The receiver now becomes the giver of the feedback.

Throughout the exercise, there should be no conversation, explanation, or justification by the receiver. If any explanation is needed, it is given after the exercise.

There are two purposes to this exercise: (1) to give an opportunity for participants to receive positive feedback from other people in an atmosphere that is conducive to sincerity and truthfulness, and (2) to develop the capacity to receive praise or criticism without generating automatic reactions that tend to be defensive or cause denial.

Many people who go through this exercise are often surprised when their positive qualities are recognized. Many learn for the first time that people appreciate certain traits that they themselves don't think of as admirable. It enhances their self-acceptance.

When the capacity to receive praise or criticism is developed, a person can listen to what is true and can ignore what is not true. This is an exercise to clearly see things as they are. Automatic push-button reactions tend to cloud our seeing or objective understanding of what is said, thus preventing us from seeing reality clearly.

Handling Worry

Worry serves a very useful function. It prods us to attend to unresolved problems. Thus, it prevents us from becoming irresponsible individuals. The problem, however, is that worry is also a major source of human unhappiness. It robs us of sleep and of the capacity to be spontaneously cheerful. It makes life heavy and burdensome.

Three factors contribute to worry:

- *Fear.* This is the root of worry. It is what makes worry unpleasant. If there is no fear, then it is a *concern* rather than a worry.

- *Unwholesome philosophy of life.* When priorities and values are unclear, then dilemmas in decision making are constantly encountered. One becomes unwilling to let go of nonviable alternatives.

- *Ineffective problem-solving methods.* This results in a lack of clarity for determining the best method for dealing with a problem. The mind tends to be dissatisfied with what is being done about it.

The first factor, fear, has been dealt with in previous chapters. The second factor is discussed in chapter 21. Here I deal with the third factor.

Eliminating Worry

These are steps that can eliminate the burden of worrying:

- *Clarify the object of worry.* When the nature of the problem is unclear, the problem can't be solved. There is a difference between anxiety and worry. Anxiety is a vague feeling, whereas worry is specific. Therefore, if anxiety is felt, its cause needs to be pinpointed. When it becomes clear, then it is converted to worry, which can then be solved.

- *Brainstorm on alternative solutions.* Brainstorming is a creative process that allows all ideas to be entertained. No suggestions are rejected, even the weird or ridiculous ones. Such apparently nonsensical ideas may give cues that lead to unconventional but effective solutions. Brainstorming is best done with other people, who can present angles or viewpoints that one may be blind to.

- *Identify viable alternatives.* After brainstorming, the ideas that are most viable are chosen. It can be one or five possible lines of action.

- *Put deadlines on each action.* Target dates for the accomplishments of these viable actions are set.

- *Accomplish the chosen actions to the best of one's ability.* The subconscious must be convinced that one's level best is being done. Only then will it cease to worry.

After having done one's best, the consequences must be accepted, whatever they are. We cannot do more than our best, even if the world crumbles down. Annie Besant wrote: "Whatever is beyond my best is no longer my duty."

Preventing Worry

As important as eliminating worry is the ability to prevent worry. Worry is a crisis that often comes from the accumulation of tasks that have not been properly attended to and resolved. Here are some ideas for preventing worry:

- Avoid doing acts that go against your principles or values. Unprincipled acts will claim their consequences later, resulting in worry and unhappiness. Thus, when you lie, you worry about being discovered.

- Write down your priorities in life. Give adequate time to each of these priorities.

- Set goals and action programs for long, medium, and short terms.

- Keep a daily things-to-do list.

- Go through your list every day, and do your best to accomplish each item, especially the unpleasant ones.

You will find plenty of extra time for the day when you have first diligently attended to your things-to-do list.

After doing your best, accept mistakes and the consequences of your choices.

Health and the Physical Body

Self-mastery is not a psychological or spiritual process that is independent of the body. Consciousness is influenced, and sometimes even determined, by the state of the body. Individuals whose brains have been damaged or have undergone surgery may experience severe alterations in their perceptions, reasoning, and states of consciousness. Certain drugs and foods, such as particular mushrooms, LSD, depressants, alcohol, or coffee, affect the state of the mind and feelings.

Effectiveness in doing almost anything in this life also depends on the state of the body. The body, when conditioned to be lethargic, often frustrates the loftiest intentions of the mind. We want to meditate in the morning, but the body's desire for the soft comfort of the bed may easily prevail over the quest for liberation. We want to help in some noble work, but the body's inertia is too heavy. We no longer control the body. Our bodies instead determine our capacity to do things.

The physical body, then, must be maintained such that it is fully subservient to the inner self, like a tamed horse that is responsive to the slightest nudges of the horse rider's reins. The body, aside from its natural needs, must not have its own acquired agenda that overpowers the more important life agenda of the inner person.

To maintain the body in an optimal condition, consider the following time-tested suggestions.

Diet

Unwholesome food is a major cause of illness such as heart disease, liver disease, and osteoporosis. We strongly recommend the adoption of a vegetarian diet for four reasons:

Health

Research has shown beyond dispute that a vegetarian diet is far healthier than a meat-based diet. Longevity studies among certain groups of people, such as the Hunzas and the Seventh-Day Adventists, show a very low incidence of the illnesses that characterize modern life, such as cardiovascular diseases and cancers. Massive studies over extended periods have produced similar results, such as a study that began in 1960 and continued for twenty-one years, among 27,529 adults in California, and another study among 11,000 people in Great Britain.[1]

In 1990, an international team of scientists announced the results of the China-Oxford-Cornell Project on nutrition, health, and the environment, which was started in 1983. This was, up to then, the largest research on diet and health ever undertaken by any group. One of its startling conclusions is as follows:

> People who eat the most animal-based foods got the most chronic disease. Even relatively small intakes of animal-based food were associated with adverse effects. People who ate the most plant-based foods were the healthiest and tended to avoid chronic disease.[2]

Compassion

Animals suffer from being butchered. Cows are sledge-hammered, axed on the head, or pierced in the throat. Do they need to suffer like this just for us to have hamburgers or steaks?

Two things are needed for an organism to feel pain: a central nervous system and pain receptors. All vertebrates—animals with backbones—have these two. This includes fish, mammals, birds, amphibians, reptiles, and, of course, human beings. There-fore, they feel pain. Every time a butcher slaughters a cow or hog for your beef or pork, conscious animals are suffering pain and sacrificing their lives for your palate. For precisely the same reasons, people don't eat their pets and compassionate vegetar-ians don't eat animals.

Animals also suffer from conditions in animal farming. Chicks in factory farms often have their beaks cut off so they don't peck at each other. (One wonders how they eat.) For months, young calves are put in pens that don't permit move-ment so their muscles won't harden. Their meat is made into tender veal. Have you ever felt it difficult to endure being bed-ridden in one position for just one day?

Effects of Certain Types of Food

Some types of food tend to disturb the body and mind, and others don't. Coffee, tea, and chili tend to stimulate the body, and other foods, such as meat, tend to make the body lethargic. Indian philosophy speaks of three types of food: the *rajasic*, or those that stimulate; *tamasic*, or those that cause lethargy; and the *sattvic*, those that are harmonious. Fruits and vegeta-bles generally fall under the *sattvic* category, and meat gener-ally belongs to the *tamasic* group. Those who seek self-mastery are encouraged to avoid *tamasic* food, whether animal- or plant-sourced.

Ecological Impact

The production of animals for food results in high environmental costs on the planet. Tropical forests in South America are being converted to grazing lands for cattle farming to supply the demand for hamburgers around the world. Forty percent of Central American rain forest was destroyed for this purpose between 1960 and 1985. A meat-based diet also contributes to the depletion of fresh water sources. The supply of fresh water in the world is reaching such alarmingly low levels that scientists are predicting future wars may be waged over the supply of water. In the United States, more than half of all water used goes to livestock production. "It takes less water to feed a vegetarian for a year than it does to feed a meat eater for a month."[3]

Exercise

The body is kept in a healthy condition when the energy system is functioning well through the proper circulation of *ch'i* or *prana* throughout all the body parts. This is done through deep breathing.

The best exercise, then, is any activity that involves deep breathing, which in turn stimulates the circulation of the energy throughout the body. Examples of these would be aerobics, *ch'i kung*, *t'ai chi chuan*, and Yoga *asanas*. The breathing process must be sustained for twelve to thirty minutes, depending on the depth of the breathing. With fast jogging, for example, the breathing tends to be very deep, and a tingling sensation is noticed in the extremities after more than ten minutes of continuous running. Sustained breathing is important, as this enables the increased circulation of the energy to reach all parts of the body.

Eastern exercises such as *t'ai chi chuan*, *ch'i kung*, and *asanas* have certain advantages over the more vigorous aerobics exercises. Because of the slower pace of the movements, it becomes possible to be aware of the parts of the body and to be conscious of the tensing and relaxing of different parts of the body.

It is important to take note of these three ingredients of effective exercise: breathing, awareness, and the cycle of tension and relaxation of certain body parts. Breathing intensifies *ch'i* energy circulation; awareness keeps one in touch with the unrelaxed parts of the body, and the cycle of tension and relaxation helps stretch and loosen parts of the body to keep them nimble, light, and agile.

Avoiding Unhealthy Habits

Certain habits or vices contribute to ill health. Cigarette smoking is the clearest example. The evidence has been so overwhelming that cigarette smoking is harmful that cigarette makers have agreed to compensate billions of dollars to the government for the medical costs of treating cigarette-caused diseases.

Drinking alcohol is another. Not only does it affect the mind, but it is directly connected with such diseases as liver cancer and cirrhosis.

Drugs have been shown to inflict brain damage on users.

CHAPTER EIGHTEEN

Attitude and Philosophy of Life

The symptoms of physical illness are but the outermost phenomena or shells of a long string of causes that are rooted in one's philosophy of life. This includes attitudes toward things and events, hierarchy of values, perspectives in life, and skills in problem solving. The following are a few examples of outer manifestations of the inner life:

- A chronic worrier is more likely to develop ulcers than a non-worrier.

- Optimistic people tend to inflict less psychosomatic damage on their bodies than their pessimistic counterparts.

- A service-oriented individual has a better immune system than one who is not.

- Laughter, as doctors have found out, can indeed be a very good medicine.

- Constant anger causes recurring headaches.

The list is a long one, showing that health is intimately connected with states of mind and feelings, which are in turn rooted in philosophy of life.

The rules of healthy living are few and simple. But we need clarity of values to know what habits to let go of in favor of better health.

CHAPTER NINETEEN

Handling Conditionings

A number of approaches have been covered that help to purify the lower triangle of unwanted conditionings and integrate any desirable conditionings that are allowed to remain. In this effort, three general principles should be kept in mind:

1. We shouldn't allow the conditionings from the past to determine present behavior without conscious consent. We grew up acquiring thousands of conditionings that we didn't have the opportunity to review and screen. Many of them are harmful and are the causes of misery and ineffectiveness. We have come to a point where we realize how conditionings control and dominate our lives. The self-transformation process has also shown that there are effective means of removing such conditionings. It is now up to us whether we will modify our conditionings or free ourselves from unwholesome ones. We must survey these conditionings and choose which ones to drop and which to retain.

2. We shouldn't allow the present surroundings and the thoughtlessness of others to determine our present state of being. When people around us are in a foul mood, does our mood become foul, too? When the weather is bad, is our mood also bad?

Consider the thermometer and the thermostat. A thermometer's mercury goes up when the surrounding temperature is hot, it goes down when the temperature is cold, and it goes up again when it is hot. In other words, the thermometer reacts according to its surroundings. On the other hand, a thermostat sets its own desired temperature. When it is set at twenty degrees C, it stops the compressor when the temperature is too cold. When it is too hot, the thermostat runs the compressor to bring it back to twenty degrees.

Now we need to ask ourselves, are we a thermometer or a thermostat? Are we helplessly conditioned by our surroundings? When someone says something nasty out of thoughtlessness or ignorance, are we enwrapped with resentment that ruins the rest of the day? Or do we determine our own state of being—our own responses to what people say or do?

Here is a verse by an anonymous author that can help us be a thermostat instead of a thermometer:

People are unreasonable, illogical, and self-centered.
Love them anyway.
If you do good, people will accuse you of selfish,
    ulterior motives.
Do good anyway.
If you are successful, you will win false friends and
    true enemies.
Succeed anyway.
The good you do will be forgotten tomorrow.
Do good anyway.
Honesty and frankness make you vulnerable.
Be honest and frank anyway.

What you spent years building may be destroyed
overnight.
Build anyway.
People really need help but may attack you if you
help them.
Help them anyway.
Give the world the best you have and you'll get
kicked in the teeth.
Give the world the best you've got anyway.

3. Undertake a program that will change your conditionings so that they will be consistent with your highest goals and values. This may be done through the following:

Regular reading of appropriate literature. Thoughts are the foundations of outer behavior and attitudes. When you regularly read chosen types of literature, your thought patterns and attitudes are changed accordingly. It is a good habit to read preselected materials on a daily basis. For example, those who feel that their attitudes are pessimistic or defeatist may wish to read self-improvement literature such as those by Dale Carnegie. Others who are inclined toward spirituality may wish to read books on meditation or mysticism.

Deliberate choice of like-minded companions. As with books, you are also influenced by the company you keep. Gossiping companions, for example, pull down thought-habits to a low personal level, further strengthening the undesirable aspects of the personality. If you have decided to seriously pursue the spiritual life, then try to seek the company of those who are already doing so.

Conscious undertaking of reconditioning programs. Self-transformation is a deliberate process. Undertake programs that will change the habits (physical, emotional, and mental) of your personality. There are many time-tested approaches. The seven-day program of the Self-Transformation Seminar is an approach to behavioral change that starts from bite-size efforts. The procedure is explained in chapter 28.

The Control of Destiny

There is such a thing as destiny. We are born into lives that have preset patterns and tendencies. That we are born to a particular set of parents and not another is part of that destiny. That we are born into a given social and cultural environment is also part of our destiny. What Buddhists call *samskaras* or seeds of karma are also part of the preset patterns of our lives, brought to us from previous lifetimes.

But such patterns and tendencies aren't rigidly fixed. Like a river, the course of the flow may be predetermined, but it can be changed. When we do nothing, then the pattern of the past takes over and our destinies are fixed. Within us are levels of consciousness that can interact with such preset patterns and hence cause a modification of these grooves.

There comes a time when we realize that the factors that determine our lives can come within our control. But we need to make a conscious choice to take control. We have the power to go beyond suffering in our lives. We have the power to change ourselves, our attitudes, our habits, and our relationships. The sooner we undertake the change in these causes, the sooner we can reap the change in the effects. Life is governed by the law of cause and effect, of sowing and reaping, of the law of karma.

When this realization comes about, we can no longer blame others for the state of our lives. We can't blame God, our parents, our president, our society, or anyone else. Not that they aren't responsible, but it is a waste of time blaming them. We may be insecure or fearful because of the way we were brought up by our parents (or whoever raised us). But that truth doesn't change the fact that we may still be insecure and fearful. We must still do something about it. And we can.

In controlling our destinies, at least three factors must be considered:

1. We must clarify in our minds what kind of life or future we wish to weave for ourselves. The development of a wholesome philosophy of life is the first step. We must be clear as to what life is all about, and we must clarify what values or principles will guide us in living it.

2. We must be familiar with the principles that govern the law of cause and effect. We must realize that we control our destiny to the extent that we control the causes of such destiny. Thus, we must not only be aware of our behaviors, but also of the feelings and thoughts that propel such behaviors. Further than that, we must be aware of the underlying roots of such feelings and thoughts.

3. We must develop self-mastery—that capacity to control the personality or lower triangle.

The various aspects of self-mastery in this section cover the most essential elements for such control. Self-awareness is its most important component.

The Law of Cause and Effect

Eastern philosophy has given to the world valuable insights about the law of cause and effect. It is called the law of karma. Below are some key thoughts for consideration.

Karma operates on all levels of consciousness. The nature of emotions and thoughts are as mechanical as the physical world, even if they are much subtler than matter. Thoughts and feelings are energies that produce effects in two directions: outward on their own planes, affecting the thoughts and feelings of others; and downward through the brain, creating a psycho-physiological pattern in behaviors.

The principle of karma affirms that when we create a thought-emotion (for they are almost inseparable), it takes on a form in the invisible world and becomes an entity on the mental-emotional plane. That entity endures according to the energy it is endowed with. Thus, an angry thought lasts longer than a passing thought about a bridge or a river. This entity is linked to its creator and needs to be neutralized at some time in the future, because it has created a state of disequilibrium. We reap our karma when an equilibrating process actively operates. In *The Mahatma Letters to A. P. Sinnett*, an adept teacher wrote that thoughts are vitalized by elementals and become active entities.

The sources of karma are from actions in this life and previous lives. The reality of reincarnation has received validation from scientific researches in the twentieth century. The issue is thus no longer a religious or theological one, but a scientific one. Those who wish to look into the matter are encouraged to read the works of Dr. Ian Stevenson of the University of Virginia. A summary of his work is succinctly stated in his essay *The Evidence of Survival from Claimed Memories of Past Incarnations,* which won the William James Award of the American Society of Psychical Research. He has gathered more than two thousand documented cases of people who remember their past lives and who were able to corroborate their claims.

There are three types of karma in every life:

Unripe Karma

This is karma that can't be equilibrated during this lifetime because the conditions are not yet suitable. Thus, if I owe a debt of gratitude to a particular individual, then I have to wait until I am reborn at the same time as that person before I can neutralize the imbalance I created in a previous life.

Ripe Karma

This is karma that is now ready for fruition in this life. Such fruition will either create more karma or it will be an opportunity for the cessation of that particular chain of karma. Thus, my enmity with an individual may lead to further hatred, thus prolonging the conflict, or it may be resolved and ended by not undertaking revenge but by processing my own feelings and attitudes maturely. This choice is open to a person who has attained a certain degree of self-awareness. Ripe karmas are divided into those that are unavoidable and those that can be avoided. Certain hereditary factors are unavoidable, like my height and physical features. Most types of karma, however, can be modified when they are blended with present karmic actions.

Present Karma

This is the new karma that is constantly being produced every hour and every day of our lives. A person lacking self-awareness mechanically produces these new karmic imbalances, whereas one who is self-aware brings this sphere of action within his or her will and control, not being mechanically driven by impulses or circumstances. It is through this present karma that we weave our future destiny. It is also through the present action that we end the chains of causes and effects coming from the past.

Some Principles of the Law

C. Jinarajadasa outlined the general effects of certain types of actions in his book *First Principles of Theosophy*. Figure 19.1 is an adaptation.

Benevolent deeds, because of their kind intent and helpful effects, generate goodwill in the hearts and minds of other people. They create an environment that is similarly benevolent to the ones who have been benevolent. This attitude or predisposition in other people may be unconscious but will nevertheless manifest in their behavior. Thus, we sometimes wonder at our fortune in receiving unexpected kindnesses from other people, even total strangers. Eastern philosophy tells us that these are

Benevolent deeds	→	Good environment
Hurtful deeds	→	Difficult environment
Aspirations	→	Ideals
Aspirations/Desires	→	Capacities
Sustained thoughts	→	Character
Successes	→	Enthusiasm
Experiences	→	Wisdom
Painful experiences	→	Conscience
Will to serve	→	Spirituality

FIGURE 19.1. Effects of Certain Actions or Experiences

not accidental. They are the natural effects of causes that we have generated in this life or in previous ones.

Hurtful deeds, on the other hand, create conscious or unconscious malevolence in other people toward the doer. Thus, it should not surprise us when new acquaintances seem to exhibit unjust attitudes and behaviors toward us, even if we have not done anything to offend them.

The workings of the law of cause and effect through many lives explain the apparent injustice in human life. We are able to see the larger tapestry of human destiny, the parts of which are woven by us day by day, life by life. This understanding brings to us equanimity when we face adversities that we are unable to prevent or correct. Neither are we perplexed when we are the beneficiaries of unexpected kindness. With this long view in mind, stretching over lives, we now realize the truth of the statement that we are indeed masters of our fate.

Response versus Reaction

When we are in a crisis or a situation that requires a decision, we may either *react* from our conditioning or *respond* with wisdom from a deeper level of consciousness. A reaction is often quick and automatic, whereas an inner response can either be slow or very quick, but always made with mindfulness. This slowness or quickness has a reason different from the quickness of a reaction. The person who has a slow response of inner wisdom may even look stupid or of low intelligence from an external viewpoint. But in the long run, and from a wider perspective, the inner wisdom response is often the wiser one.

We need to distinguish the use of reaction and response here. A *reaction* refers to the behavior triggered by a stimulus upon a *conditioned* pattern, such as when we automatically jump at the sight of a frog or get angry at the thought of a person. A conditioned pattern is triggered, and the reaction is automatic.

A *response* is an action that arises from a deeper evaluation of the situation by the higher mind, with or without intuition. The higher mind is free from personal likes and dislikes, fear and desire, and attraction and revulsion. It assesses situations based on values or principles and from a more complete perspective, with minimal distortion from personal conditionings.

For example, suppose we are insulted in the presence of

other people. A typical reaction is feeling humiliation, then anger, then perhaps aggression (or timidity). Some push buttons have been triggered, and the reactions are automatic.

On the other hand, if we don't have any push buttons (no patterns of reaction to an insult), there will be no anger or feeling of being humiliated, although we may not be oblivious to the fact that the other person is aggressively attacking us. This understanding of the action of the other person is absorbed and understood in the higher mind or the deeper levels of consciousness, and a non-conscious assessment happens. The resultant behavior of that inner assessment is what we shall call response. Even if we have push buttons to the insult, such as feeling angry, we are still capable of inner response, so long as we have an awareness of the anger.

Skill in Action

A response may be combined with outer skill in dealing with the situation. In the example above about being insulted in public by someone, we might just remain silent, since we are unaffected by the verbal abuse. Or we might decide to say something that could effectively deal with the situation. Saying something effectively entails interpersonal skills that involve verbal fluency, familiarity with attitudes and emotional reactions of people, and familiarity with cultural customs and values.

When such outer interpersonal skills are combined with inner assessment, then a response tends to be wise, and can even be swift, if necessary. Its action can be faster than a reaction.

The feats of some martial arts practitioners, such as catching an arrow in flight with the hand, offer striking illustrations of the swift response that arises out of this inner assessment and outer skill. Reaction alone won't produce this skill, as a reaction is too slow for this. Reaction moves from a fixed pattern, and hence it can't respond well to unexpected situations.

The capability to respond, instead of react, requires the development of a transparent outer personality (body, emotions, and lower mind) that doesn't obstruct the immediate perception of the situation by the higher mind. The higher mind is capable of quickly synthesizing the disparate aspects of a situation much faster than the logical mind. Because of this, it is able to respond to the situation quickly and effectively when combined with outer skill.

The Gap between Perception and Response

As an exercise to develop the daily capacity for deeper response rather than superficial reaction, one should be conscious of a gap between perception and response. The gap may be a fraction of a second or it can be thirty seconds, depending on the urgency of the moment.

When a fire breaks out, for example, it is wise to pause for a few moments and be aware both of the situation and of one's own internal state: tension, fear, confusion, and so on. Those few moments—say, five seconds—won't substantially delay the subsequent action (unless lives are critically in danger at that moment), but they can enable one to act more wisely in doing the important things rather than reacting mindlessly in a panic. I have seen people go into a state of shock upon seeing a fire, thus becoming a liability more than a help, because other people have to attend to them. This is sheer uncontrolled reaction. Being aware of the gap between perception and action can be practiced in many small ways in daily life. For example, when the phone rings, be aware of any unthinking automatic reaction to answer it.

I have earlier spoken of the "telephone meditation" of the Buddhist monk Thich Nhat Hanh when receiving phone calls. In making phone calls, he suggests further that the following verse be read before dialing:

> Words can travel many thousand kilometers;
> They are to build up mutual understanding and love;
> I am determined that my words will be beautiful
>   like flowers,
> I vow that my words will be beautiful like embroideries.

Paste the poem on your phone to help you become mindful while talking on the phone.

We can invent many ways to remind ourselves to be aware of reactions in daily life. A mother who is constantly irritated when the bathroom is dirty can put a sign on the door of the bathroom to remind her to be aware of herself as she inspects the bathroom. When she sees that it is messy, she can be aware of any rising irritation—not suppressing the irritation, but being aware of it. That moment of awareness is the needed gap between perception and action.

When we cease to be reactive, and outer appropriate skills have been developed, then this deliberate gap becomes unnecessary. Action is then swift and spontaneous, in addition to being wiser.

Clarification and Integration of Values

The philosophy of life for every person consists of two aspects: (1) a map of reality—an understanding of what life is all about, of nature and the cosmos; and (2) a hierarchy of values—a perception of which things are more important than others

The philosopher Will Durant wrote that wisdom is "seeing big things as big, and small things as small." This implies that, first, we see reality objectively, rather than in a distorted way, and second, we see the relative importance of things.

Clarification of values means that we must review which values should guide our lives. *Value* means what is worthwhile. If happiness is worthwhile, then it is a value. If giving time to the family is worthwhile, then it is a value. If playing basketball is worthwhile, then it is a value.

The problem starts when these values conflict with each other and compete for our time and attention. Between family and basketball, which one is more important? Between honesty and earning more money, which one is more important?

When we don't give time to the consideration of this point, then our *conditioned values* take over. They subconsciously dictate what is more important and what is less important. Thus, a father spends more time with his office mates than his family after work, although when he is later asked about it, he realizes that his family is more important to him than his friends.

Kinds of Values

There are three kinds of values: universal, cultural, and personal.

Universal Values

Universal values are valued by all human beings because of the intrinsic nature of these values or by virtue of our being human beings. Truth, for example, is valued for its own sake. We want to know the truth rather than be misled or be under an illusion. We prefer an illusion only when there is fear or psychopathology, in which case we then put the value of avoidance of pain over that of truth. But even in the latter case, it is not because we don't prefer truth to illusion.

Happiness is sought by every human being because of our biological, psychological, and spiritual makeup. Even masochists inflict pain upon themselves because they derive happiness from it.

Universal values are shared by human beings regardless of culture and age. The following are some of these universal values: truth, happiness, inner peace, love, kindness, justice, respect, courage, and fearlessness.

Schools universally espouse these values. But the problem is that schools and teachers don't take them seriously. They recognize that they are often impractical (such as honesty) and almost unattainable (such as happiness or inner peace). Thus, universal values are seen as ideals. Modern society gives evidence to the prevalence of values that contradict these universal values. We look into this conflict in a later section.

Cultural Values

Cultural values are dependent on the social norms, religious beliefs, and other environmental situations of people. Thus, in a society in which the ratio of males to females is just one to ten, polygyny may be legal and ethical; if the reverse, polyandry may be the legal and ethical custom. In some countries, divorce is permitted, in some it is a sin.

Some cultural values are cruel and yet are tolerated or even promoted by members of the community. For almost a thousand years in China, prior to 1912, many women were subjected to the binding of the feet with cloth to make their feet small and dainty. This resulted in the breaking of the toes and the deformation of the entire foot. Girls from three years old onward were subjected to this cruel practice by their mothers, and they underwent severe pain for two or more years. The practice was prohibited when Sun Yat Sen founded the Republic of China.

Cultural values also change with time. What was unethical in one generation may no longer be so in the next. Many of our attitudes and beliefs are derived from these cultural values and hence are conditioned values. Cultural values are not necessarily good for humanity. We need to review such values, because they can create inner and outer conflicts.

The tendency to accumulate wealth, for example, is a very strong cultural conditioning derived from society's measurement of success or from family expectations. We may not have fears or strong desires that impel accumulation, but our minds subconsciously assume that it is the preferred value, and because it is an embedded or hidden assumption, it is often unquestioned. It then exerts pressure on us and can become exceedingly influential or even overwhelming in view of its unquestioned validity. It can effectively overrule any decision we make to adhere to universal values.

A review of our cultural values is thus a review of our philosophy of life. Few people do this deliberately. It requires a broadness of knowledge about life and human affairs.

Personal Values

Personal values are worthwhile to a particular individual and differ from person to person. Thus, some people may value art more than earning money and thus spend more time painting, even if it provides little income. Others may value money more than art and thus spend more time buying and selling paintings than being painters themselves.

Personal values are largely subjective and are neither ethical nor unethical, except when they go against one of the universal values. Thus, whether we prefer chocolate or vanilla is a subjective preference. But whether we eat the flesh of a mammal can be an ethical issue, because it now touches on the pain and suffering caused by the slaughtering of animals for food.

It is important to realize that *inner peace is not possible if our personal values contradict one or more universal values.* True inner fulfillment eludes us because we can't integrate the higher and lower aspects of our being.

If I do an injustice to someone while trying to earn money, I won't have inner peace. I will feel insecure. More important, I intuitively know that it is a *wrong* thing to do. This sense of unethical action doesn't come from cultural values but is due to an inner sense of right and wrong that we have, regardless of our culture. Thus, it is important to explore a way of life in which universal values are in harmony with personal values.

Are Universal Values Practical?

In my talks, I sometimes ask the audience (some of whom are schoolteachers) who among them believes that honesty is the best policy. Perhaps half of them or fewer raise their hands. When we ask how many of them consider that honesty is practical, usually one or two, or none at all, raise their hands.

We are facing here a fundamental contradiction between our principles and our daily reality. It seems impractical to be honest or to be truly principled. We believe that we can't rise in our careers if we are honest or if we don't compromise with the demands of the environment that compel us to lie. Or we can't win an election if we are too honest, or become a successful salesperson unless we exaggerate or misrepresent the product. How true is this widespread impression?

Principles and Achievement

Many years ago, I read a book by Joe Girard, who was listed in the *Guinness Book of World Records* as the Top Salesman in the World for at least seven consecutive years. Girard was a car and truck salesman. Sometimes customers would come to him to buy a special kind of vehicle that his manufacturer didn't produce. He would tell the customer that his company didn't have that vehicle, but that it was available from another manufacturer (a competitor), and Girard would even refer the customer to the competitor's dealer. But he would also tell the customer that if in the future the customer needed anything that Girard had, then they should call him. He would then give the customer his card.

Such honesty had an effect on potential customers. People from across the continent called Girard if he could supply them with what they needed, and if Girard had it, he stood a good chance of getting the order, because he had been honest with the customer. Girard didn't rise to the top through insincerity and manipulative tactics.

I knew a lady entrepreneur who was one of the material vendors of a huge public works project in the Philippines. The public works buyers discovered that among their suppliers, this lady was apparently the only one who didn't overprice or connive with other suppliers to pad their quoted prices. In time, the buyers developed so high a trust in this lady that they would ask her to help them check the prices of items they were buying. Needless to say, this lady received large orders from this public works project, simply because she was honest and trustworthy.

One public official, Jesse Robredo, whom I knew very well, took the road less traveled and was determined not to succumb to corruption when he was elected mayor of a city in the Philippines. Group after group came to him offering regular amounts of money if he would just agree to look the other way. Time and again he politely declined, until the syndicates found that they were facing a mayor who was dead earnest about his principles. Unlike other politicians, he didn't include journalists and media people in his payroll just to ensure that they said good things about him or to be silent about anything they observed to be wrong. It didn't take long for the people to realize that they had in their midst a truly honest official. They gave him their trust. He won by a landslide in every reelection, with little campaign funding to sustain him. In one election, he ran unopposed. Three years after he stepped down as mayor, he was awarded the Ramon Magsaysay Award (the Asian Nobel Prize) for government service, the first local official ever given such a recognition. He was later appointed Secretary of the Interior and Local Government, a position he held until his untimely death, when the private plane he rode crashed into the sea. The nationwide expression of grief upon his death made him something like a people's hero.

I can cite many examples of people who, when they are clear about their values and have developed mature skills in management and interpersonal relationships, excel in their respective fields and reach levels that are unattainable by people who employ deception or are insincere. There are millions of politicians, but only those who are principled earn the name statesman. There are many so-called religious people, but only a small percentage are called spiritual.

Stephen Covey, in his best-selling book *Seven Habits of Highly Effective People,* noted that truly successful individuals are those who are *character-ethic* oriented rather than the *personality-ethic* oriented. The lives of character-ethic-oriented people are guided by principles rather than by conveniences, by what is just and compassionate rather than what is selfish. The personality-ethic-oriented individuals may bribe or be insincere in order to achieve a certain goal, but their success will be blocked by walls that can only be surmounted by adherence to universal principles. They may soon discover that they have paid for their shortsighted "success" with a high price.

Values in Daily Life

The test of the practicality of universal values lies in our daily life applications, which I will presently explore. Most parents lie to their children, and many do so habitually. Why is dishonesty necessary with our own children? Why can't we even be truthful with the people closest to us? Many parents justify their dishonesty by saying that they tell white lies for the good of their children. But I wonder what is good about having parents who can't be trusted?

This is a typical example: A young son approaches his mother and asks for money to buy something from the store. The mother feels that her son doesn't need it, so she says that she has no money. The boy is disappointed. As he goes into another room, he hears his father ask for money from his mother, and the mother replies, "Just get it from my brown purse."

If you were the son, what would you feel? How will you take your mother's words in the future? Do you think that the white lie of the mother was worth the potential resentment and distrust felt by the son?

Part of the problem is that the mother didn't realize that it was possible for her to say no to her son and to give her sincere reasons without necessarily creating resentment in her son. This option would have been less harmful than lying, even if the boy felt disappointed with her "no."

To be sincere requires the capacity to communicate assertively and sincerely. We must also have developed the self-awareness to be able to face discomfort in our feelings. Your friend comes grinning and proudly shows you her new hairstyle. She asks you, "What do you think of my hair?" You happen to think that it doesn't look good at all. In fact, you think she looks ugly with it. What do you say? In many cultures, it is proper to say, "It looks OK" or "It looks nice," even if it is a blatant lie.

By learning how to communicate assertively, we can have a better idea of how to give feedback without being judgmental, to speak truthfully without unnecessarily hurting the other person.

Taking Bite-Size Efforts

In the quest for self-transformation, we need to experiment with daily opportunities to integrate universal values in our lives. Do it at a comfortable pace.

For example, try bite-size honesty. Using assertive communication skills, take risks in being truthful in small daily things. With these modest victories, you can gradually find it easier to be truthful in many things in daily life—with your children, spouse, friends, peers, office mates, and others.

Experiment with bite-size justice and fairness. When you forego an unfair advantage, you may find that you can take the apparent sacrifice. It also feels good deep inside. Again, with such small victories, you will find it is no longer difficult to be just when it comes to large matters.

Do bite-size kindnesses every day. Say "thank you" to people whom you don't usually thank for small favors, like passing the salt. It gradually becomes a habit. You will no longer even think of it. The "thank you" just automatically comes out of your lips whenever anybody does any small thing for you.

Clarifying Personal Values

To integrate universal values into your life, you must do another necessary task: clarify your own personal values. Many of us go through life not knowing that our personal values are not really our own. They are just reflections of the demands of our surroundings: our parents, friends, society, and what people will say. We begin to wonder why we are not happy in our careers or why we easily get angry when we are performing our work.

Winnie worked as a legal researcher in one of the best law centers in the country for about twenty years. When I met her, she said that she was due to retire in two years. Seeing that she was still young, I asked her what she planned to do after her retirement, thinking that she would set up her own law practice. She said, "I'll open up a dress shop." I was caught by surprise, and I couldn't say anything for a few moments. I asked her why. She said, "Ever since I was young, I have always wanted to design dresses and make them. Now that I'm about to retire, this is the thing that I really want to do."

"Then why did you become a lawyer?" I asked.

"When I was entering college, my uncle wouldn't finance my studies unless I took up law. So I did."

"If that's really what you want to do, why do you have to wait until you retire before you do it? Why don't you do design and make dresses during weekends?"

She paused for some moments, then thoughtfully said, "Yes, that's a thought. I had not thought of that option."

It has been more than ten years since that evening, and I haven't met Winnie again. I often wonder what she felt throughout the twenty years when she was doing legal work. I wonder what she is doing now. I wish that she is happy in her new career, doing creative designs.

Would you and I be willing to devote more than twenty years of our lives to something that we didn't really love? Lack of clarity of our personal values can condemn us to a life that we don't cherish, to a work that we don't find fulfilling. It is essential for each one of us to clarify what is truly meaningful in our lives—things that we would like to live and even die for.

To help attain such clarity, try to answer two questions. They may be difficult to answer; nevertheless, do your best. You can always change your answers later. I suggest that you *write down* your answers, not just think about them. Writing them will force you to be specific and to see your present hierarchy of personal values more clearly. The first question is: *what are three things that you would like to do or achieve or become before you die?* Write them down in the order of their importance. The second question is: *what are three things that you would like to do or accomplish within the next three years?*

In answering the first question, you are really searching

for an answer that doesn't come from your outer self, which is your logical mind or emotions. When your outer self answers, you might reply according to the values of society, which may not resonate with your innermost self. You want the answer to come from somewhere deeper within you.

For this reason, it is important to review the list after a week, a month, and a year. See whether your answers are still the same. If at these different times your list is the same, you may be reasonably sure that you are hearing the answer of your deeper self. If the list keeps changing, then it means you are listening to your outer self.

Your answer to the second question helps you determine whether you will be spending your coming years meaning-fully. If what you do for the next three years has got nothing to do with your lifetime list, then decide whether you are doing the right things for the next three years or, on the other hand, whether your lifetime list needs to be revised.

Check also whether your personal values are in harmony with universal values. If not, review them and see whether, deep within yourself, they are really what you want in life.

Internalization of Values

The above discussion and exercises constitute the first, but nec-essary, stage in the internalization of values and behavior. The second stage is the integration of these values. Two things are required to internalize values: (1) universal and personal values are clear. You must be convinced that universal values are valid and truly worth pursuing, and also that your personal values are clear and strongly felt; and (2) contrary conditionings are neutralized.

The conditionings to be neutralized are of two kinds: (1) physico-emotional conditionings—those involving habits and emotional reactions, such as fears and resentments; and (2) mental conditionings—those molded by cultural values, such as the measurement of success and failure and philosophy of life. They create preferences for lifestyles, modes of action, and so on. This aspect is related to a review of your map of reality. When true clarity is achieved and conditionings are comprehensively reviewed, then values can be fully integrated into your life with minimal difficulty.

Integration and Capability Building

The self-transformation process includes a stage in which the ego is strengthened to enable it to deal with the pressures and threats of the environment. Strengthening the ego includes what may be called capability building in the broadest sense. It is the strengthening of each level of consciousness (such as the development of mental, emotional, and physical skills and capabilities) and the integration of the contents of these levels according to a set of priorities.

When the ego isn't strong, we have a tendency to withdraw, to regress, or to be defensive. This delays further the path toward full maturity of the individual, because self-actualization and self-transcendence are impeded by these self-defensive reaction patterns.

Let's look at some illustrations of this weakness.

Interpersonal Relationships

Timidity and low self-esteem are examples of ego or personality weaknesses that lower one's overall capability. Timid people are hesitant to assert their rights or dare even to ask questions or inquire or clarify. The root of this is, of course, fear. It is the outcome of conditionings from childhood.

An aggressive and boastful person is free from this weakness, but aggression creates its own internal and external distresses. In contrast, assertiveness is not subject to the pendulum of timidity and aggression. Assertiveness is another level of interpersonal interaction that is effective and at the same time not productive of new conflicts and distress. In this example, capability building is from timidity to assertiveness, bypassing aggressiveness as an intermediate learning stage.

Problem-Solving Capability

Life requires the capacity to understand problems and to resolve them. This is usually a rational capacity that includes knowledge, analytical power, and clarity of thinking. Some people don't seem to have the mental energy or the training to undertake persistent mental activity to solve a problem. In other words, the mental body or structure is weak or underdeveloped. It is essential that such a capability is first developed, because unless it is, the result is low self-esteem that will further reinforce the tendency to be timid, resulting in further ineffectiveness in life.

When people resort to methods such as astrology to solve their problems, or to explanations such as karma and past life as a justification of what is happening to them, they may sometimes think they have outgrown their problems, but actually they are still in a state of inadequate maturity, looking for a convenient shortcut to the quandaries of living.

I have often observed, for example, that many people resort to fortune-telling in order to face or solve their problems. I am concerned not with the accuracy or falsity of the particular fortune-telling approach, but with the person's motivation to seek answers in this way. Fortune-telling offers bundled solutions or explanations to problems. The answers are more understandable—"Your aunt will get well in three months" or "You will meet a person who will be your husband." But to depend on the answers of another person, fortune-teller or not, is an abdication of decision-making powers and the capacity to guide oneself through one's own future or destiny.

Paradox

Now we face an apparent paradox: the highest stage of the self-transformation process is egolessness, but structure building is strengthening of the ego. Aren't we building something that we have to destroy later?

Strengthening the personality is a stage that we must go through prior to transcendence. Weakness of the ego leads to regression into the fragmented state (discussed below) instead of transcending toward the spiritual state.

The transpersonal psychologist Ken Wilber quotes an author who states that eighty percent of New Agers who claim to pursue the transpersonal are actually back to the prepersonal, that is, they are actually regressing back to a defensive, secure sanctuary as a reaction to their incapacity to deal with their present social and cultural environment. Wilber himself thinks that not more than one percent of the people in the world are at the spiritual stage.

The importance of the development of this intermediate

stage can be found in the writings of spiritual classics and of notable people. Gandhi is reported to have said that it is better to be violent than to be nonviolent out of cowardice. True nonviolence originates from a position of strength and transcendence rather than weakness.

In the *Bhagavad Gita*, Arjuna refuses to wage a battle with his cousins and prefers to be killed rather than to kill. Krishna, Arjuna's spiritual teacher, "realizes that what Arjuna considers his revulsion from the act of killing does not stem from spiritual realization but from cowardice."[1] Swami Prabhavananda comments that "Arjuna has not yet reached the spiritual enlightenment which would permit him to renounce action. To fight is his duty, dictated by his character which his past thoughts and actions have imposed upon him."[2]

The spiritual classic *Light on the Path* states: "Seek in the heart the source of evil and expunge it. . . . Only the strong can kill it out. The weak must wait for its growth, its fruition, its death."[3]

All the above quotations exemplify the need to go through a period of capability building before we can attain a transcendent stage.

Stages in the Process

There are three recognizable levels in the self-transformation process: the fragmented, the integrated, and the transcendent levels. These are correspondent to, but not necessarily identical with, what transpersonal psychologists refer to as prerational, rational and transrational or prepersonal, personal and transpersonal. Wilber's works dwell at length on this distinction, and I recommend his writings to the interested reader.

Fragmented

This is a stage in which the different parts of the consciousness function somewhat independently and often conflict with one another. The rational faculty is not yet capable of integrating the different aspects of the personality. It is expected that as we mature, these different parts will become integrated. In many people, however, this integration doesn't occur as they grow up, leading to what Wilber calls dissociation, instead of differentiation. Differentiation is richness, whereas dissociation is pathological.

When there is fear or hurt, for example, these emotions react independent of reason and may overpower reason. These emotions, behaviors, or tendencies may be contradictory to each other. Thus, a father may believe that he loves his son, yet he is capable of inflicting punitive pain on the son. A person may be convinced that seeing a doctor is important, and yet delays the appointment due to fear.

A symptom of the fragmented level is ineffectiveness in affairs such as work, relationships, health, and inner peace. The ineffectiveness may be pervasive and covers almost all major facets of life (as in the case of an alcoholic), or it may just be in one facet, such as the marital relationship. This is caused by the structures of the psyche not being integrated, and priorities and values may not be clear.

When one is fragmented, then it is necessary to undertake what is sometimes called a structure-building program to strengthen the integration of the personality with the rational faculties. Push buttons such as fears and unwholesome needs and desires should be processed and neutralized. A hierarchy of values and priorities should be clarified. The will should be strengthened.

Integrated

The result of a good structure-building program is integration and leads to the enhancement of the effectiveness in the affairs of one's life.

The immediate purpose of the self-transformation process is such an integration. We assess which aspects of our lives are not working well and then undertake a program to improve those aspects. The methods used should not be palliatives, but should lead to permanent effectiveness. Thus, in a strained relationship, avoidance is a temporary solution, whereas self-awareness, listening, and effective communication are permanent solutions. In sleeplessness, pills are palliatives, whereas awareness and normalization of stresses lead to an enduring solution to the problem.

Integration makes us *capable* in a worldly sense. Whatever work or responsibility we choose to do or to accept, we are generally effective and efficient. If it is a skill that we need to learn, then we will have no hesitation in acquiring the skill the best way we can.

Transcendent

This is the next stage of growth, in which the spiritual consciousness and intuitive wisdom play growing roles in one's life. An awareness emerges that goes beyond the rational. This is the highest level of maturity. In itself, the transcendent stage is characterized by multiple substages recognized in mystical literature. I shall cover this topic more thoroughly in chapter 23.

Structure Building

Integration involves the efficient interconnectedness among different aspects of the personality and the higher individuality, such as the following:

- Values and priorities are clear, such that when one perceives a conflict in a situation, there is little hesitation to decide in favor of a certain direction that will be consistent with one's highest values, even if there is apparent sacrifice in terms of more basic needs, such as physiological or financial needs.

- Unwanted push buttons are no longer dominant. They are subservient to higher reason. The higher will is now superior to the desires of the lower triangle of the personality. Whenever there is a conflict between the will and the desires or needs, the will prevails more often, if not always.

- The rational faculty is healthy. One can recognize fallacious reasoning and is able to see others' points of view, whether agreeing with them or not. Muddled thinking is minimized, such as using feelings and reasoning for issues that primarily need reasoning to resolve.

In the self-transformation process, structure building involves the following components:

- Self-awareness processing: minimizes tension, stress, and the various conditioned push buttons in the subconscious that cause emotional distress and confused thinking

- Self-mastery: the capacity to carry out what is perceived to be the highest choices of the rational faculty

- Effective relationships: the capacity to deal effectively with human conflicts

- Seven-day program: practice in strengthening the will over the desires

- Self-inventory: a self-assessment of what is working and not working in one's life as an indicator of what structure to strengthen in the ego

Aspects of Structural Integration

The integration process involves internal coherence within a structure (intrastructural), such as reason, and between structures (interstructural), such as between reason and emotion.

Intrastructural Integration

The first aspect of integration is within each level of consciousness. Many individuals, for example, harbor contradictory beliefs and are not even aware of it. This is especially evident when it comes to religious beliefs. Many people believe that

God is all-merciful, and yet they harbor the belief that there is eternal damnation when they die guilty of some mortal sin.

This is often because of the lack of motivation to clarify intellectual issues and beliefs. It is symptomatic of an undeveloped mind, a weak mental capacity. It is characterized by a low mental energy level. A deliberate effort to read, discuss, and write helps to strengthen such mental weakness.

The same internal fragmentation is seen in emotional natures. Pendulum-like moods represent the contradictory emotional states that one may have in the same situation or environment.

Interstructural Integration

The second type of integration is between structures. A person may be convinced that smoking is injurious to his or her health and should be abandoned (mental belief), and yet the individual's body may be addicted to it and can't give it up (physical inclination).

These interstructural contradictions are common among the majority of humanity. Our educational systems often don't systematically deal with these problems and may even frequently nurture them. The same goes for parenting. This is because both parents and teachers harbor these same contradictory tendencies within themselves.

Integrating these fragmented parts of the psyche involves first a recognition of what they are—contradictions—and then adopting approaches to make them congruent. It entails the permanent disappearance of one (or both) of the contradictory tendencies or beliefs. It also entails strengthening the view or behavior that is most consistent with reality.

Transcendence

The highest realm of human experience lies in the transcendental. It goes beyond sensing, feeling, and thinking. The terms *mystical, spiritual,* and *transpersonal* refer to this realm.

We eventually reach a point in our lives when we experience an emptiness or a yearning that can no longer be satisfied by physical, emotional, or mental experiences. Reason is no longer adequate. What we call human happiness is no longer enough. Such a dissatisfaction is sometimes described as the divine discontent. It is an unquenchable thirst until we "come home" to our true origin. Thomas Merton, the well-known Catholic mystic, wrote, "The spiritual anguish of man has no cure but mysticism."[1]

Transcendence is not a one-time experience that, when attained, is permanent. The word covers a multitude of levels of attainment. Mystical literature refers to two general levels: illumination and union. They are equivalent to the realization of the *buddhi* and the *atma,* or enlightenment and nirvana. Each of these levels has sublevels of attainment.

Mysticism

Mysticism has been defined as the quest for "union with the Absolute,"[2] or "a spiritual quest for hidden truth or wisdom, the goal of which is union with the divine or the transcendent realm."[3]

Mysticism, according to Evelyn Underhill, the well-known author of the classic work *Mysticism*, "is not an opinion; it is not a philosophy. It has nothing in common with the pursuit of occult knowledge." Every major religious tradition has its mystical element, often described by a distinctive term representing a distinct tradition with that religion. Thus, in Islam, it is called *tasawwuf* or Sufism; in Judaism it is called Kabbalah. In Christianity, it is often referred to simply as Christian mysticism. In Hinduism, there are many mystical schools, but the more popular ones are Raja Yoga and Vedanta. These schools are often identified with the name of the person who first expounded their teachings, such as Ramana Maharshi for *vichara* or self-inquiry and J. Krishnamurti for choiceless awareness. Buddhism also has diverse mystical traditions, such as Tibetan Buddhism and Zen Buddhism.

The mystical quest is characterized by stages, with substages within each stage. Western writers such as Evelyn Underhill consider that the major stages are as follows:

- Awakening

- Purification of the self

- Illumination

- Purification of the soul

- Union

Awakening

Awakening refers to the call of the inner self when the divine discontent is felt. It is the true spiritual conversion, not merely one that changes labels. Geoffrey Hodson calls it "the call to the heights."[4] In Islam, it is the real *tawbah* or conversion, not just a declaration of faith. One feels that there is a deeper meaning to life than the worldly life of the senses. This awakening leads to a search for the true path, or the valid and time-tested way to realize the transcendent. The awakened spirit intuitively finds the right one, for it feels the inadequacy of those paths that merely satisfy the personality. In Islamic Sufism, the path is called *tariqah*.

Purification of the Self

The *purification of the self* is the removal of the conditionings, desires, and unwholesome needs of the personal self or the lower triangle. This is necessarily a long process. The later this is started in life, the more difficult is the process of purification. So much garbage will have already been acquired that the pain of purification could be intense. This cleansing process is the beginning of the path. The great mystical traditions have laid down the guidelines that throw light on this dim road. It involves self-denial, because the self has acquired so many desires and needs that are obstructive of the spiritual life.

Self-discipline of the personality is required at this stage.

We see now the true significance of the so-called moral commandments or ethical codes: the *yama* and *niyama* of Yoga, the *paramitas* of Mahayana Buddhism, the avoidance of the seven cardinal sins in Christianity, the guidelines in *At the Feet of the Master* by J. Krishnamurti or those of the *Vivekachudamani* (Crest Jewel of Wisdom) of Sankaracharya. In Islam, the purification process is the real or greater *jihad* or holy war. It is the conquest of the self. It leads to the different *maqams* or spiritual stages.[5]

Illumination

Illumination is the glimpse of the larger reality, of the transcendent. It often refers to a sudden experience of enlightenment. It is the awakening of the *buddhi* or *prajna*, the spiritual consciousness. In Zen, it is the experience of *kensho* or *satori*. It can sometimes manifest in a life-shaking cosmic consciousness.[6]

But the dawning of the mystical consciousness can be gradual and imperceptible. It can start with what H. P. Blavatsky calls *manas-taijasa*, or mind illumined by the *buddhi*. As the *buddhi* becomes a part of daily consciousness, it is referred to in Christian literature as the contemplative consciousness, or "the presence."

The illumination stage has its many substages, such as the various kinds of *samadhi* in Yoga. In Sufism, they are the *ahwal* (singular, *hal*), or spiritual states.[7]

Purification of the Soul

The *purification of the soul* is the growth process after the spiritual consciousness has begun to be active in one's life. Like the preceding stages, it also has substages and facets. Modern transpersonal psychology and psychiatry have identified various conditions that arrest the growth process in one's spiritual life. Classic mystical literature, both Eastern and Western, is replete with guidelines for this stage. St. John of the Cross wrote of the "dark nights" of the soul and the senses. Buddhism speaks of the ten fetters that must be overcome until one has become a full *arhat*. The spiritual initiations in theosophical literature speak of these same fetters.

Union

Union refers to the merging of the individual consciousness with the divine consciousness. It is called *fana* in Islam and nirvana in Buddhism. One might think that such a state is the final attainment of the soul, but the different traditions again speak of various degrees of union. Thus, aside from the nirvana of Buddhism, there is still *paranirvana*, or beyond nirvana, as well as *Mahaparanirvana,* or the great beyond-nirvana. In Islam, *fana* has several degrees: *fana' fi ashshaykh* ("annihilation in the master"), *fana' fiar-Rasul* ("annihilation in the Prophet") and *fana' fi-Allah* ("annihilation in God").[8]

For the average individual, the self-transformation process mainly involves self-mastery, which is concerned with the purification of the personal self, whereas transcendence is concerned with cleansing the higher mental consciousness and preparing for the awakening of the higher levels of consciousness.

Seeing What Is

When you see a drawing of a provocative object, such as a gun, what is your immediate reaction? I have asked this question to hundreds of people while projecting on a screen the image of a drawing of a pistol. The typical answers are violence, death, blood, fear, threat, and power. After they have given their reactions, they are told, "Has it occurred to you that this is a sheet of cloth (the screen) with shadows cast upon it? When you react with fear or anxiety, or you think of death and blood, you are reacting not to *what is* but to the associations you give to what you see. You are therefore really reacting to your memory, not to what you see. In what you see, which are but light and shadows and a cloth, there is no violence, no threat, and no death. We therefore don't see *what is* in our daily life. We constantly see our memories."

To see "what is" ought to be the simplest of acts. In practice, it is extremely difficult. In fact, it is one of the hardest things to do in life because we can't help but see with our conditioned minds. Whenever we recognize anything, then we are seeing it according to the label or the purpose or function of that object, based on what we were taught.

A chair is never that "thing" there. When we see it, it is always a chair with functions, designs, and degrees of comfortableness.

The same happens when one sees a husband, wife, or children; or sees words, buildings, and any familiar object. Even with an object that we have never seen before, we try to classify it or compare it according to what we have known before.

This faculty of the intellect is very useful. It enables us to navigate effectively through the natural world as well as in the social world. But this capacity has its disadvantages. It also becomes our prison. When the label and associations of an object are established in the mind, then it develops an automaticity that almost always prevents us from seeing outside the associations. Thus, to some of us, a syringe is always to be avoided, for it is painful. It hardly occurs to us that it may be a blessing, for it is the best way of bringing medicine speedily into the body.

The problem arises when the object becomes linked to some emotional reaction like pleasure or pain, like or dislike, attraction or repulsion, love or hatred. It is immensely difficult to be free from such an imprisonment in perception. We only see what is presented by our intense reactions. We no longer see the thing as it is.

What we call self-realization, spiritual maturity, and perfection all necessitate developing this capacity to see things beyond the conditioned structures of perception. It is to see things as they are, regardless of whether we like them or not, appreciate them or not, need them or not. It means, then, that we must be able to see this reaction pattern; otherwise, we will not be able to free ourselves from it. We can only liberate ourselves from something when we see what it is that imprisons us.

To see the walls of this abstract prison, we must cultivate

a sensitivity that can watch the movements of our subjective experiences—thoughts, motives, feelings, and ideas. We must be able to see them without judgment, for judgment is in itself one of those things we need to watch.

Thoughts, memories, and associations prevent us from seeing things as they are. In exploring this capacity, therefore, we must be able to watch our thoughts as we look. This eventually develops the quality of nonattachment even as we recognize the value of a thing in the eyes of the world.

Evelyn Underhill refers to this capacity as having the "simple eye."[1] J. Krishnamurti calls this "choiceless awareness," an awareness that simply looks without labeling, judging, choosing, or identifying.

To see with the simple eye doesn't mean that we lose the capacity for labeling or remembering associations. The capacity of the intellect to do this is certainly a useful one. We can't return home from the workplace without this faculty; neither could we recognize a spouse or children. In being able to see things as they are, however, we are not trapped by this ordinary cognitive level of perception. We are capable of seeing things not merely on one level but on multiple layers of reality.

The Illusory Nature of Perception

When we reflect on our perception of things, it becomes evident that what we are seeing has an illusory nature. A few examples may suffice.

Things appear to us as they do because we happen to be equipped with visual instruments (our eyes) that perceive the color spectrum, from red to violet. This band of light waves from red to violet is but a minuscule part of a very wide span of the entire electromagnetic spectrum that includes radio waves, infrared waves, ultraviolet waves, x-rays, cosmic rays, and gamma rays, all of which are invisible to us. If it so happens that our eyes could only see in the range of x-rays, we would be seeing bones and organs instead of skin and clothes. Beauty would be measured no longer in terms of facial features but in terms of the most attractive bone shapes.

The scale of our vision also determines our valuation of an object. For example, we see a "smooth" skin because we see at a scale that makes us virtually blind to the irregularities of the skin cells. If our vision were microscopic, like the way the eye of a fly sees, what we would see is skin hairs, the oil secretions, the surface bacteria, and the holes of the skin. We might have second thoughts about kissing those things.

But the illusory nature of our perception isn't limited to the physical senses. It extends to the subtleties of emotional and mental interpretation of things. In the same way that our visual perception is locked within a certain range, so the way we "feel" and "think" about things is also locked within certain ranges, according to our emotional and mental instruments. Reality is far beyond these limited ranges.

To see things as they are is a subject that has received attention in psychology since the time of Sigmund Freud. In psychoanalysis, Freud encourages a free-floating attention that is not focused. In concentrating one's attention, the mind tends to follow the inclination of one's expectations and thus will not see things as they are. Here is an interesting statement by Freud:

If one's expectations are followed in this selection there is the danger of never finding anything but what is already known, and if one follows one's inclination anything which is to be perceived will most certainly be falsified.[2]

Note the striking parallelism of this statement with a recurrent theme in the talks of J. Krishnamurti:

The mind . . . has functioned always within the field of the known. Within that field of the known there is nothing new. . . . To put that question, we must be tremendously earnest because if we put the question with a motive, because we want certain results, the motive dictates the answer. Therefore we must put the question without motive, without any profit; and that's an extraordinarily difficult thing to do.[3]

The totality of our conditioning is the known, and that conditioning can be broken, but not through analysis.[4]

Commenting on Freud's view, Abraham Maslow stated:

Freud recommends passive rather than active attending on the grounds that active attention tends to be an imposition of expectations upon the real world. Such expectations can drown out the voice of reality, if it be weak enough. Freud recommends that we be yielding, humble, passive, interested only in finding out what reality has to say to us.[5]

Maslow further warns against our "rubricizing" what we perceive—classifying, cataloguing, pigeonholing, or stereotyping—rather than seeing things in their naturalness and uniqueness. "Rubricizing perception . . . is an invitation to mistakes."[6]

Meditation

Meditation is the time-tested means toward inward exploration of consciousness. It helps us discover the subtle prison walls of the mind that prevent us from seeing reality as it is. It is the gateway to the discovery of the true Self.

The term *meditation* is used for a wide range of practices. We must be able to distinguish spiritual meditation—or classical meditation—from the rest.

For example, the Silva Method by José Silva is called meditation, but it is different from spiritual meditation. The Silva Method involves the reconditioning of the lower triangle. It enables a person to easily become relaxed or to attain the alpha state of brain activity.

Spiritual meditation, however, is concerned with the fuller realization of the higher triangle. To do this, the meditator tries to make the lower triangle become serene.

This observation can also be made of Transcendental Meditation and Relaxation Response as they are popularly practiced. These methods have proven their usefulness and effectiveness in bringing about changes in the personality. They can be used in conjunction with spiritual meditation, but they are different from spiritual meditation.

Spiritual Meditation

Spiritual meditation assumes a background philosophy or outlook that questions the assumptions of life as lived by the average person. It sees the mundane world as but an outer layer of a much vaster reality. This mundane world is often characterized by conflicts that lead to sorrow and pain. Spiritual meditation doesn't seek to escape from such a world, but rather, to transcend it. What follows is a description of the practice of spiritual meditation.

Meditation seeks the awakening of the transcendent consciousness, preceded by a series of preparations that make it possible to go beyond the personality, that is, the physical, emotional, and mental levels of consciousness. Such a meditation is not primarily involved with images or visions or voices. Where there are images or shapes or recognizable objects or colors, then it is still in the realm of concrete thoughts. Meditation seeks to transcend these.

The object of preparation is to allow the lower triangle, or the personality triangle, to be serene. After preliminary preparations are done (body, emotions, sensory perceptions, etc., discussed below), we work toward inner tranquility by applying the steps described in the following sections.

Concentration

Concentration systematically disciplines the mind by reconditioning its habits. The use of a mantra is one way to discipline the mind. A chosen mantra or word is used as an anchor. By mentally repeating it over and over again, usually following the rhythm of the inhalation and the exhalation of the breath, the mind is disciplined to ignore things other than the mantra, thus gradually developing an attitude of disinterest in extraneous things not chosen by the meditator.

Concentration is a necessary step in Raja Yoga as described in the *Yoga Sutras* of Patanjali. The counting of breath in Zen is another example of this disciplinary stage.

Awareness

Awareness involves watching the movements of the mind, including feelings, reactions, and ideas, as well as the origin of these movements. Such awareness brings about a calmness of the personality triangle, thus freeing the consciousness to be aware of subtler realms. Examples of this approach would be the "choiceless awareness" of Krishnamurti, the mindfulness of Buddhist meditation, and *vichara* or the self-inquiry meditation of Sri Ramana Maharshi.

Meditation involves an unenforced awareness of the contents of the consciousness. In concentration, there is a struggle between the intention of the meditator and the conditioned habits of the mind. In meditation, this struggle ceases, and the consciousness uninterruptedly maintains an awareness of whatever is in the mind.

The meditation process then enters into the realms of *samadhi* when the center of consciousness, the observer, loses its separateness from the object of its attention. The wall that divides itself from the object melts away.

Both these approaches are used by meditators. Eventually, however, all meditation leads to the awareness stage. Concentration or other modes of disciplining the mind are but preparations for awareness meditation.

Preparations for Meditation

A classic approach to meditation is outlined in the *Yoga Sutras* of Patanjali, written about 2,500 years ago. Despite the terseness of its aphorisms, it contains perhaps the most comprehensive map of the transcendent consciousness. It remains the outstanding text to this day on the subject.

A valuable part of the *Yoga Sutras* pertains to the preparations needed for the attainment of *samadhi*. Patanjali outlines the seven stages of preparation, which culminate in the eighth, *samadhi*, characterized by the *cessation of the modifications of the mind-stuff.* Each of the seven stages is concerned with specific aspects of our nature that prevent us from attaining *samadhi* and awakening *prajna*, or intuitive consciousness. An overview of these preparations is helpful here (see figure 25.1).

1. Restraints (*yama*). These are five behaviors that eventually contribute to integration and the absence of internal psychological conflicts: nonlying, nonviolence, nonstealing, nonsensuality, and nonacquisitiveness. Their opposites are behaviors that are rooted in psychological needs and desires that automatically disturb the mind.

2. Observances (*niyama*). These are five attitudes or qualities of mind that eventually lead to self-transcendence: purity, contentment, simplicity, self-study, and self-surrender.

3. Proper posture (*asanas*). In entering into the meditative silence, the body must be steady and comfortable so that it doesn't become a source of disturbance. The best

Higher Self (Atma)	Nirvanic consciousness; Union
Transcendent (Buddhi)	*Samadhi, Satori,* Illumination
Higher Mind	*Dhyana* (*Zen, Ch'an*) Meditation: Awareness
Lower Mind Uncontrolled thoughts/memories Disturbances from the senses	*Dharana*: Concentration *Pratyahara*: Sense withdrawal
Emotions Fear Anger Anxiety and worry Greed Ignorance Egotism	*Yama* (Restraints) Nonviolence, nonlying, nonstealing, nonsensuality, nonacquisitiveness *Niyama* (Observances) Purity, contentment, simplicity, self-study, self-surrender
Etheric Double Tension/nervousness	*Pranayama*: Breath control
Physical Body Pain and discomfort	*Asanas* (postures) and Hatha Yoga

FIGURE 25.1. Attaining Equanimity through Meditation. Based on the *Yoga Sutras* of Patanjali, this figure shows how the meditative life (right column) deals with disturbances in the lower levels of human consciousness (left column, lower part) in order to attain equanimity.

posture for meditation is probably the full lotus position. Other alternative postures are the half-lotus posture, the sitting posture, and the kneeling posture.

4. Control of vital energy (*pranayama*). This vital energy, called *prana* or *ch'i*, circulates to all parts of the body throughout the day. When unregulated, it can be a source of disturbance in the mind. The control of the energy is done through regulating the breathing. Notice that inhalation and exhalation have an effect on thoughts. Hence, the eventual diminution of the breathing activity during meditation results in minimal stimulation of thoughts from pranic activity.

5. Sense withdrawal (*pratyahara*). The mind is then withdrawn from the reports of the senses. The reception of light, sounds, and other sensory stimuli by the senses can't be avoided. It is automatic. But the perception of these sensory reports can be withdrawn by the mind. Thus, when one is reading an absorbing novel, one may not notice that a door just banged or that cars passed by. The ears continue to receive sensations, but the mind has not entertained them, that is, the mind was withdrawn from these sensations. Sense withdrawal refers to the act of the consciousness withdrawing from all sensory reports.

6. Concentration (*dharana*). This means focusing the mind on a chosen object. It trains the mind to be under the direction of the will of the meditator. The mind of the average person is a slave to external stimuli and

psychological conditionings. It thinks according to these circumstances. Concentration is a practice that regulates this undisciplined tendency.

7. Meditation (*dhyana*). The uninterrupted dwelling of the consciousness on its object is meditation. While concentration involves enforced discipline, meditation naturally dwells on the object without being distracted or disturbed.

8. *Samadhi*. This occurs when the distinction between the object and the meditator has ceased. Only the object now remains.

The above is but an outline of the eight stages. I recommend that you look into a deeper understanding of the process by studying the *Yoga Sutras* themselves with the help of commentaries, such as those of Dr. I. K. Taimni in his book *The Science of Yoga*.[1]

Dealing with Thoughts in Meditation

Meditation seeks to attain a state of awareness that is not absorbed in thought processes. It is a state of being, rather than thinking, in which the malleable mental stuff (*citta*) ceases its almost endless modifications. Yoga calls this state *samadhi*.

On the road to such a state, we encounter various mental conditions that effectively become obstacles to the cessation of *citta*. We need to be aware of these intermediate states and learn how to deal with them.

In reading the sections below, keep in mind that the end state we seek is pure awareness without content—pure subjectivity that is nondirected and effortless.

Initial Approaches

Each time you enter into meditation, it is essential that you take note of the state of the mind. Is it filled with the noise of the day? Is it peaceful? Is it stressed? The meditational approach that will be helpful sometimes depends on these initial states.

For example, when the mind and body are tense and still reeling from the problems of the day, a Mantra Yoga approach may be helpful just to calm the mind. This makes use of words or focus points that allow the mind to dwell on one thing rather than be carried away by jumpy thoughts. The word or words constitute the auditory focus, and the visual focus can be any spatial point or activity.

I recommend that you begin your meditation with the repetition of a two-syllable word such as *Soham* ("That am I"), *Hamso* ("I am That") or their English equivalents. You can also say "one two," or even mentally count from one to ten. Let these words follow the pattern of your in-breath and outbreath. The first syllable is mentally uttered when you breathe in, and the second syllable is uttered when you breathe out. Breathing is normal. At the same time, focus your mind on a point somewhere in your head, such as the area between your eyebrows. Do this mechanically until your thoughts move away from events and concerns. An alternative spatial area of focus is your in-breath and outbreath.

The repetition of a one-word syllable such as "Om" can also be used. Mentally recite the word during exhalation. Be aware of the thoughts in between the recitation of the word. Alternate words can be "*Mu*" (meaning "nothing") or "One."

Thoughts

In dealing with thoughts, it is helpful to recognize the various levels of thinking, which are images and sounds, abstract thoughts, and intentions.

Images and sounds. The first group consists of gross thoughts. Observe them until they calm down naturally. Mental chatter belongs to this class.

Abstract thoughts. When the train of images and the chatter of the mind cease, then be aware of formless thoughts. These are the abstract thoughts that are subtle but imperceptibly swift in their movements. Recognition of things or objects or concepts is a movement on this level. That is, the moment you recognize anything, such as a chair, even if you don't call it a chair or identify it verbally, there is already a subtle movement in the mind. Be aware that the process of naming, recognizing, and subtle judging is going on all the time. Awareness tends to slow down this automatic activity. You become aware of the space in between these thoughts.

Intentions. A special kind of abstract thought is intention. Intentions seem to emanate from nowhere—just popping out into the field of consciousness. You think that you voluntarily choose these intentions until you discover that they just appear without your willing them. Note, in fact, that the belief that intentions are voluntary is illusory.

Behind all these is the energy that pervades consciousness—or perhaps *constitutes* consciousness. The energy is not distinguishable from the consciousness. When the energy disappears, consciousness also dims and disappears. You become asleep or unconscious.

When this energy remains, there is awareness. The object of meditation is to maintain this awareness without being identified with any of its contents—thoughts, motives, perceptions, and so on.

The Self

Finally, the consciousness may enter into a state of bare subjectivity, of bare awareness devoid of intentions, recognition, preferences, and naming. This state can easily be lost by the slightest perceptions from the senses or the slightest wisps of memories. Gradually, through practice, the length of time this state can be sustained increases.

This state is like rich soil, where germination or gestation occurs under the ground unseen. A contemplative process goes on imperceptibly, leading to the emergence of a subtle substratum of consciousness that remains even during nonmeditative periods. It is the "presence" that mystics speak of, the emergence of *prajna*, or of the *buddhic* consciousness.

Attaining this substratum of consciousness is a significant development in the practice, because it is the link between the transpersonal and the personal in one's daily life. In fact, it is the emergence of the transpersonal in daily life.

Whatever is happening—while you are working, thinking, reading, feeling, reacting—this substratum is a nonparticipating but influencing witness. It influences because by its very presence it prevents certain unwholesome things from happening, such as tension, suppressed emotions, and automatic reactions.

Barrenness

There will be times when apparently nothing is happening during meditation. You must not assume that nothing is *really* happening. Meditation, as mentioned above, is like planting a seed in the ground. You water it every day, and yet nothing seems to be happening on the surface. However, underneath the surface, unseen, the seed is germinating and sprouting. One day, a bud comes forth, silently, slowly, imperceptibly, that eventually grows into the luxuriance of the plant.

Self-Transformative Effects of Meditation

The regular practice of meditation has a cumulative effect on the consciousness, character, and personality.

First, it helps expand the field of peripheral awareness, those contents and perceptions of the field of present consciousness that are outside the field of attention and awareness. This peripheral awareness begins to become part of one's general awareness. The effect is integrative, that is, the contents and perceptions of the peripheral awareness don't remain as independent elements of the consciousness that might eventually result in psychological conflicts and distress. If we become aware of subtle discomforts, we stay with the experience of discomfort until it is resolved, either through processing or reasoning, but not through repression.

As the field of peripheral awareness expands to subtler levels, we become aware not only of feelings or discomfort, but also thoughts, motives, attitudes, prejudices, or preferences that react automatically to perceptions or stimuli. This is good. They are part of the conditionings carried by the subconscious mind. This expansion of awareness accelerates the dissolution of the push buttons in the subconscious. It is thus a working partner of self-awareness processing in dealing with the fragmentation of the lower self.

Perceptions, recognitions, or stimuli can be likened to a ping-pong ball that enters the field of consciousness. When the field of peripheral awareness is narrow, the ball immediately hits walls of the subconscious, with all its push buttons, and bounces off immediately, that is, elicits immediate and automatic reaction. This bouncing is unpremeditated, unprocessed, and not the result of mature reflection.

When, however, the field of peripheral awareness grows deeper, a different sequence of events happens. The ping-pong ball travels farther before hitting any wall, and thus slows down. If it hits anything at all, the bouncing will be less forceful. If it doesn't hit any wall, then it just slows down to a stop, and floats there until it dissipates. When the peripheral awareness is deep enough, then the coming of the ping-pong ball is noticed by a deeper layer of consciousness—the illumined mind (*manas taijasa*), or the *buddhi* itself. The perception by the illumined mind or the *buddhi* results in an understanding that leads to a subtle response that is now translated by the personality into action (which assumes that the higher and lower triangles are now seamlessly integrated).

Second, the practice of meditation opens the channel between the brain consciousness and the transpersonal consciousness. In the average person, this channel is occupied by the ego or the personal self, with all its connections with the subconscious. Not much from the subtler levels can pass down to the grosser levels. The ego, with all its insecurities, wants to take charge.

In creating a larger peripheral awareness, meditation expands this channel or bridge and, at the same time, deflates the ego. This enables the light of the higher consciousness to filter down into the ordinary waking mind. As we process the concerns of the ego more and more, it becomes thinner and more transparent, becoming less of an obstruction to the descending light from the higher realms. In Yoga, this is described as the state of *samapatti*, when the self is like a transparent jewel, no longer distorting the surrounding realities. Patanjali says that with this, there is the dawning of the spiritual light into the consciousness.

Samadhi and Enlightenment

A special aspect of meditation, samadhi, needs to be touched upon in view of the vagueness that usually clouds an appreciation of it. *Samadhi* is often equated with enlightenment in many writings. To the best of my understanding, this is not accurate. Enlightenment is a form of samadhi, but not all samadhis are the equivalent of enlightenment. In the same manner, *samadhi* and *satori* in Zen are not synonymous.

Samadhi, as a term used by Patanjali in his *Yoga Sutras*, is characterized by the *absence of the observer* in relation to an object of attention. Out of this state, *prajna*, or "intuitive knowledge," may emerge. What is normally understood as enlightenment is the presence of samadhi plus prajna. Prajna is the insight, or knowledge, from the buddhic or spiritual consciousness.

Samadhi involves a structural change in the consciousness, but enlightenment involves an intuitive awakening: awakening of a transcendent faculty of perception that enables one to see things in their *is*-ness.

It is not necessary for samadhi to occur before the light of prajna filters into the ordinary mind. When the insights of this higher faculty, or *buddhi*, filter into the abstract mind, then the mind itself can be said to be illumined—the *manas taijasa*, or "radiant mind."[2]

Intuition

It is unfortunate that the word *intuition* has become confused with hunches and extrasensory perception. True intuition is neither of these, although in its manifestation it may make use of these other faculties of the psyche. Intuition is a transcendent faculty of perception. It integrates whatever is experienced by the other senses or whatever lessons are learned from the past, but it adds another level of perceiving reality that is beyond reasoning, emotions, and sensations. Intuition sees the essentials of a situation and of things, and incorporates deep universal values when assessing a situation that needs response or decision. It is a faculty that everyone should endeavor to awaken within oneself. It entails deep awareness and the capacity to be inwardly quiet in order to perceive the subtle nudges of intuition.

Intuition is the equivalent of prajna in Eastern mysticism. Christianity doesn't have special equivalent terms to *prajna; intuition* and *spiritual perception* come close. The word *contemplation* has been employed for this purpose, but it tends to drag the meaning farther away because of the word's association with thinking and deliberation. The word *faith* has similarly been used for this, but the word is so heavily laden with other connotations that again it covers more than it unveils.

The Essential Unity of Religions

The study of spiritual consciousness and mysticism makes evident that there are several important layers in every religion:

- The outermost layer consists of the *rituals and ceremonies* of a religion. These are obviously superficial in nature and do not represent the heart of a religion. These rituals frequently change.

- The next layer is the theology of a religion, consisting of each religion's set of *beliefs or doctrines*. These too are often subject to change. Catholicism, for example, has changed its dogmas over the course of centuries. It has modified its view about the belief that the earth is the center of the universe or that there is no salvation outside the church.

- The innermost layer is spirituality, or the *mystical or spiritual aspect* of a religion. In this layer, there has been hardly any change in the past several thousand years when it comes to the essence of spirituality. Spirituality is experiential, and each generation of spiritual seekers tends to validate what has been previously discovered or realized. Mysticism is the heart of every religion. It is the flame that keeps a religion alive and makes it survive disastrous mistakes that theologies and rituals may make.

This explanation can be represented by a series of concentric circles, as shown in figure 26.1. The outermost circle are rituals and ceremonies. The next circle is the theology of the religion. The third circle is spirituality, or the mystical core of religions.

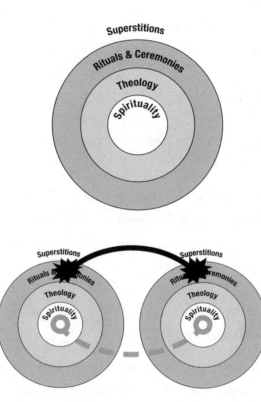

FIGURE 26.1. The Universal Layers in Religion.

Religious groups easily find themselves in conflict with others when they define their own group in terms of rituals, ceremonies, or theologies. When, however, they define themselves in terms of spirituality or mysticism, they find themselves in harmony with the mysticism of other religions.

This third circle consists of many subcircles, such as gnosis or esotericism and the different degrees of mystical attainment. Outside these three layers, we find the superstitious beliefs that accrue around every religious tradition.

When religious adherents focus mainly on the rituals or theology of their own religion or those of others, they have a tendency to regard each other with suspicion, with separateness, and even with hostility. The religious violence that we see in the world is the result of living the religious life on those two outer levels. In Ireland, we see the strange phenomenon of Catholics and Protestants, both Christians, bombing and killing each other. In the Islamic world, we see Shi'ites and Sunnis killing each other. How people of the same religion can be so divided that they turn and kill each other is indeed an astonishing phenomenon. What seems equally astonishing is that many people take this for granted, as if it is nothing to feel strange about. A visitor from outer space studying humanity would surely find the human species a curious one.

But among the mystics of the great religious traditions, we don't find such enmity, suspicion, separatism, and hostility. The Vedantists, the yogis, the Sufis, the contemplative Buddhists, the Christian mystics, the Jewish Kabbalists—they see more things that unite them than things that separate them.

Thomas Merton, the well-known Trappist monk who has written best-selling books on the spiritual life, was one of those who delved into the essence of the spirituality of various religions and compared them. In a book entitled *Zen and the Birds of Appetite*, he asked whether a Catholic can practice Zen and remain a Catholic. He answered with a definite yes. Zen, to him, is an experience and not a dogma. It is not different from the spiritual experience of a Catholic or a Protestant.[1]

A Catholic nun from Canada, Sister Elaine MacInnes, wrote a book entitled *Teaching Zen to Christians*.[2] She considers herself a disciple of the Zen *roshi* Yamada Koun while remaining a Catholic nun. She established the first Zen center in the Philippines and taught numerous nuns, priests, and laypeople the practice of Zen meditation. How can a Catholic nun—a disciple of Christ—be at the same time a disciple of a Zen Buddhist *roshi*? This is possible only if we see the essence of Zen spirituality as being no different from Christian spirituality.

Hazrat Inayat Khan, the Sufi teacher who popularized Islamic mysticism in the West, stresses the essential unity of the spiritual experience among the different traditions. He in fact declared, "No one can be a mystic and call himself a Christian mystic, a Jewish mystic, or a Mohammedan mystic. For what is mysticism? Mysticism is something which erases from one's mind all idea of separateness, and if a person claims to be this mystic or that mystic he is not a mystic; he is only playing with a name."[3]

Mahatma Gandhi, when asked what his religion was, said that he was a Hindu, a Muslim, a Jew, a Christian, and a Buddhist.

Abraham Maslow, in his book *Religions, Values, and Peak-Experiences*, wrote:

> To the extent that all mystical or peak-experiences are the same in their essence and have always been the same, all religions are the same in their essence and always have been the same. They should, therefore, come to agree in principle on teaching that which is common to all of them, i.e., whatever

it is that peak-experiences teach in common (whatever is *different* about these illuminations can fairly be taken to be localisms both in time and space, and are, therefore, peripheral, expendable, not essential). This something common, this something which is left over after we peel away all the localisms, all the accidents of particular languages or particular philosophies, all the ethnocentric phrasings, all those elements which are *not* common, we may call the "core-religious experience" or the "transcendent experience."[4]

This realization about the essential unity of the world's religions is the real solution to the interreligious strife that the world has been witnessing for millennia. It is not just a wish or a hope. Interreligious harmony already exists among the mystics of all religions today. It is only among those who see their religious life in terms of dogma and rituals and organizations that there is hostility and separation. To help in attaining religious unity, we must popularize the mystical and spiritual aspects of religions.

The Unity of Life

The transcendent consciousness brings out another insight into the nature of things—the unity of life. This is the ultimate foundation of universal brotherhood. Let us explore this more deeply.

Look at a single leaf of a tree. Its life appears to be separate from the other leaves. The apparent proof of such separateness is that if we cut that leaf, it will die, but the other leaves will not die or be injured.

Yet look again. What gives life to the leaf? It comes from the nourishing sap that passes through the twig, the same twig that supplies the same life to the other leaves. In other words, the leaf doesn't have a separate life. There is only one life that animates not only the leaves, but also the twigs, branches, trunk, and roots of the entire tree, which are but the outer garments of that life. The garment withers and dies during autumn and winter, and a new garment springs up in spring and summer. The garment changes, but the life doesn't. It is the same one life. The leaves look separate, but they are really but one life.

Look at your fingers. They are also separate. You wound the small finger and you feel the pain, but the other fingers aren't bleeding. They remain healthy and unaffected. And yet these fingers don't have separate lives. They are part of the one life that runs through the entire body of the human being. The separateness is superficial.

We see other human beings as separate from us. If you feel pain, I don't feel it. If you die, I don't die. Indeed, it seems true that we are separate. But that is because we are identifying ourselves with the outer garment that we call the body or personality. If we look deeper into our human nature, a different realization may dawn upon us. Among those who realize this inner unity of life are the mystics, whose consciousness of the higher self, or higher triangle, has awakened. In them, there is a natural emergence of not only compassion, but a realization of the unity of life. There is but one Life, of which we are individual expressions. These manifested egos identify themselves with the garments that they temporarily wear, and thus think that they are separate. But one who has awakened to the inner recesses of one's consciousness becomes aware of the unity of life.

Is it any wonder that St. Francis of Assisi wouldn't even step on ants when he walked? That he considered the sun and the moon as his brother and sister?

John Donne had a mystical insight when he wrote these immortal words:

> No man is an island, entire of itself; every man is a piece of the continent, a part of the main. If a clod be washed away by the sea, Europe is the less, as well as if a promontory were, as well as if a manor of thy friend's or of thine own were: any man's death diminishes me, because I am involved in mankind, and therefore never send to know for whom the bell tolls; it tolls for thee.

Corroboration

This concept of unity in organisms and nature is now gaining wider acceptance in scientific circles. In biology, the theory of morphic fields and morphic resonance is one example; the Gaia theory of the earth as one organism is another; Carl Jung's collective unconscious in psychology is another example. Arthur Koestler propounded the concept of holons, a view that has been adopted by transpersonal psychologists such as Ken Wilber. A holon is a whole unit or organism that is also a part of a larger whole. Everything is a holon; that is, each thing is composed of smaller parts, although it is itself a part of a larger whole. A holon is equivalent to Rupert Sheldrake's morphic unit. The whole series of holons forms a hierarchy of holons, or a holarchy.

Collective Unconscious

One of Jung's major contributions is his theory of the existence of the collective unconscious, a level of consciousness shared in common by all of humanity. Its manifestations are in the forms of myths and archetypes.

Jung said, "The collective unconscious . . . is not individual but common to all men, and perhaps even to all animals, and is the true basis of the individual psyche."

Morphic Resonance

Sheldrake propounded the theory of morphic resonance in 1981 with the publication of his book *A New Science of Life*. Everything—that is, every *morphic unit*—whether atoms or crystals, organs, animals, social systems, or the entire cosmos itself, has its own *morphic field*. These fields determine the form and behavior of the unit or organism, because the fields have *memories*, and the forms and behavior follow these memories. These fields can be behavioral, social, cultural, or mental. They constitute the underlying unity of organisms as well as the interrelationship between different organisms, which may be part of a larger morphic unit.

Similar morphic units affect each other through a process that Sheldrake called *morphic resonance*. For example, ten rats in England may learn to solve a new maze in ten hours. This learning is said to have an effect on other rats that may be thousands of miles away, such that rats in the United States may solve the same maze in a shorter period. Experiments have been conducted that appear to validate this hypothesis.

Although Sheldrake is careful not to say that this implies a common consciousness, he does say that it is something similar to the concept of Jung's collective unconscious. In a television interview with Dr. Jeffrey Mishlove, Sheldrake was quite explicit about this:

> MISHLOVE: When you talk about these fields containing a memory, they almost begin to sound like the mind itself, in some funny way.

SHELDRAKE: Well, if they're like the mind, they're much more like the unconscious mind than the conscious mind, because we have to remember that in our own minds, a large part of the mind, as Freud and Jung and others have told us, is unconscious. And what Jung and his followers have emphasized is that not only do we all have our own personal unconscious, but we also tune in to or access the collective unconscious, which is a collective memory of the species. What I'm saying is very like that idea, but it's not confined to human beings, it's right through nature.

The idea of animals of a particular species sharing conscious-ness is equivalent to the concept of a group soul in Theosophy. By extending this concept to human beings, it means that there is a larger shared field, or consciousness, among human beings. As Sheldrake said, "In the human realm this is similar to Jung's theory of the collective unconscious."

The Seven-Day Program

We come now to the concluding portions of the self-transformation process. We have covered a wide spectrum of information and practice. Assuming that the reader has tried the exercises given in the previous chapters, we are now ready to explore two approaches toward continuous self-transformation in our lives.

The first is the seven-day program, and the second is the "Next Step," which is discussed in chapter 29.

The seven-day program is a specific step toward the strengthening of self-mastery. Using the various methods and approaches covered in this book, select a particular behavior in your life that you would like to change (add, improve, or remove) for the next seven days. It should be something that is done almost on a daily basis, rather than something that is only done once a week. Examples are to stop smoking, to exercise every day, to minimize anger, to undertake a diet, and to read every day.

In choosing the behavior, keep four criteria in mind:

1. *Specific.* The seven-day program involves a specific behavior, not just a vague general wish. For example, decide not

simply "to be more healthy" (too vague and general), but rather "to do *tai chi* for thirty minutes every morning," or "stop smoking," or something else of your choice.

2. *Measurable.* At the end of the seven days, you must be able to determine whether you have accomplished your program or not. Thus, if you wish to minimize anger, then you have to estimate how often or how intense you get angry every day or every week. If it averages four times a day, then you may wish to lessen such occurrences of anger to not more than once a day. (Note: You must also be clear as to whether you are including irritation in your definition of anger.) Or you may measure your anger in terms of intensity, not just frequency. On a scale of zero to ten, what is your average level of anger?

3. *Somewhat difficult.* It should be a behavior you have avoided doing—in other words, something you have been resisting so far. You shouldn't choose a seven-day program for something that you are already doing regularly. The program is concerned with the strengthening of the inner will and the mastery of the outer personality. But don't undertake a program that may be very difficult, one that you are likely to fail. The purpose of the seven-day program is to strengthen your inner will as opposed to the desires and inclinations of the outer personality. Every time the inner will prevails, it gets stronger. Hence, try to achieve bite-size victories. When you start a seven-day program, make sure that you will do it. If you don't really intend to carry it out, then don't undertake the program,

otherwise you will subconsciously lose faith in your own willpower.

4. *Methodical.* A method must be chosen to ensure that you will successfully accomplish the seven-day program. For example, suppose that a father would like to spend more time with his children instead of working overtime in the office. Then he must plan a work schedule and a reminder to ensure that he doesn't get worried about any unfinished work. He may wish to delegate part of his work to others, or change his client appointments to noontime instead of dinner, or ask his wife to help by calling to remind him at a certain time in the afternoon. If the seven-day program is to lessen stress, then have a reminder to do scanning, say, four to eight times a day. The reminder can be the watch or other objects that you have the habit of looking at several times a day. Every time you look at the watch, then check your level of discomfort. If it is three or above, then do scanning for a few minutes.

Aids to the Program

Remember that the seven-day program is basically a reconditioning process. Therefore, you can make use of well-known techniques of influencing the subconscious mind to support the effort. Following are two such methods that can strengthen the seven-day program.

Strengthen motivation. This is an approach suggested by author and motivational speaker Anthony Robbins. The purpose is to create leverage that will propel you to act on your seven-day program.

On a sheet of blank paper, draw a vertical line down the middle, dividing the paper into two columns. In the left column, write down the *advantages* or *benefits* to you if you are able to accomplish your seven-day program. In the right column, write down all the *disadvantages* or *harmful effects* if you don't do your seven-day program. Write down as many reasons on both columns as possible.

Visualize. Another technique is visualization. Here is an approach adapted from a method used by José Silva.

Suppose your seven-day program is to wake up at five o'clock a.m. and meditate for twenty minutes. You can use visualization to help influence your body, feelings, and mind to be more inclined to implement your resolution.

Close your eyes and breathe in deeply five times, until your whole body is relaxed and your feelings are calm. Then imagine yourself behaving in your old way (feeling lazy about getting up). Put this picture or scene in a frame that has gray-colored borders. Now picture yourself briskly getting up and doing your meditation. Put this scene in another frame, superimposed on the first picture. The border of this frame is a bright golden color. Keep this framed image in mind for at least two minutes. Feel the calmness and the benefits of meditation while you visualize yourself meditating.

Visualization is a powerful tool for reconditioning, and for this reason it must be used with care. What we consciously or subconsciously visualize in the mind tends to condition our personalities to behave according to such images.

Self-Transformation Group

Participants in the Self-Transformation Seminar are encouraged to meet regularly afterward so they can form a growth group that will nurture and continue the transformation process. The group meets weekly or monthly on an agreed fixed day, and there is an agenda for the gathering that includes talks, exercises, or discussions that add to the members' growth. It can be a study session led by an assigned discussant, or a processing session, or a structured learning session. If you have not attended such a seminar but feel that you would like to explore and implement some of the approaches you find in this book, then you may like to form an informal group of friends who are similarly interested. You can, for example, discuss together one of the chapters in this book, and then explore its relevance to your lives and decide on what each person wants to do about it. You can devote one meeting every month to self-awareness processing to deal with any accumulated tension or cleanse past push buttons or address emotional issues.

The members of the group can also undertake common service work that transmits the fruits of their own learning to other people who can benefit from them, particularly young people who are groping in the dark about what life is all about.

The Next Step

To a person who has consciously started the self-transformation process, the opportunity for growth and transformation becomes a continuing one, no matter what the circumstances are. One important factor in the acceleration or slowing down of this process is, among other things, the availability of the *energy of awareness* to sustain the process.

At every stage of life, there is a *next step* (or steps) toward growth. This next step can be found by asking yourself questions such as the following:

Am I tense right now?

Am I uncomfortable in any way?

What aspects in my life still make me unhappy?

Am I strongly dissatisfied about something? What can I do about it?

What relationships in my life still don't seem to work?

Are there worthwhile things that I like to pursue but I seem to hesitate to?

Are my priorities and values in life clear to me? Are my
activities in accord with these priorities?

Do I feel fulfilled in my work?

Do I find life to be meaningless or directionless?

Am I complaining about anything in my present
circumstances?

Every circumstance that presents a conflict, a sorrow, or a
dilemma, whether major or minor, represents a potential *next
step* in your growth. Conflict and pain indicate the lack of integration and transcendence. They are the clues to both the problem and the solution.

The approaches or methods that we have explored in the
self-transformation process are the means by which you can
take that next step that you hope will lead to resolving and
surmounting the conflict.

Karen had been familiar with the self-transformation process for more than a year and had processed a lot of issues in her
life already. In fact, she volunteered to train as a facilitator for
the seminar. When I next met her, more than a year after she
had been introduced to the process, she told me that she had
entered into a new business. One evening prior to a meeting,
I asked her how she was doing in her new business. She said,
"I'm dead." She saw that I didn't understand what she meant.
She explained that she felt so tired and exhausted that she felt
like a dead person. And this wasn't just that evening. This had
been an ongoing ordeal for her for about a month. The stress,
the physical exhaustion, the arguments and disagreements, all

these had been draining her every day so that she wanted to give up the whole business.

It surprised me that it hadn't occurred to her that this torment she was undergoing is what the self-transformation process is meant to address. She perhaps assumed that business problems are different from self-transformation issues. This is a mistake. Nothing is outside of the self-transformation process, because the process is about living itself. Whether it is a toothache, or an irritation, or a trauma, or the impending death of a loved one, everything is part of the growth process and hence relevant to self-transformation.

Karen was going through the distress and agony due to a couple of factors: she accumulated daily stress and forgot to normalize it regularly, and she hadn't formulated a clear philosophy of life that encompasses such things as businesses and problems.

We discussed the matter, and I reminded her of the use of self-awareness in dealing with problems like this. She smiled, acknowledging that she had forgotten. I saw Karen again several times during the next week, and she felt that her days were going much better. She was less tense and enervated at the end of the day.

Let's look at some examples of the almost infinite possibilities of the next step.

You are about to take a long bus or plane ride. In the past, you normally felt tired or exhausted after the long trip. This upcoming trip can be the next step. As you begin the trip, notice whether your body is relaxed and comfortable. Do scanning and check for any discomfort or tension. It won't be difficult to see that if you can ensure that you are comfortable at this moment and can maintain it throughout the trip, then a twelve-hour trip won't be exhausting. A trip is only tiring when you maintain a tense position for long hours.

You are waiting for some people, and they are late. You are becoming bored and impatient. Let this impatience be the opportunity for the next step. Be aware of your impatience and fully experience it, without trying to remedy the discomfort or justify the lateness of the other people. Do abdominal breathing as you scan yourself.

You and your spouse have a recurrent point of conflict. It causes hurt feelings and raised voices. The next time it arises, try listening to the point of view of your spouse without giving your own. Allow it to sink in, and endeavor to understand the feelings and attitude behind the words. (Note that to understand others doesn't mean you agree with them.) Allow yourself to experience with full awareness the conflict within yourself, even if nursing the conflict takes the whole day. If there is anger within you, feel it with awareness. After you have processed these feelings and returned to a state of equanimity, you will be ready to discuss the issue with your spouse effectively. If you have been at fault, it will not be difficult for you to apologize. If your spouse is at fault, you will be able to discuss it without anger or resentment.

You are worried about a task that needs to be done, but you keep procrastinating about it. Stay with the worry and be aware of the conflict within you. Don't push it aside. Be aware of the unpleasantness. Be aware of the reasons you are postponing the task. Process yourself if there is a strong emotional reason behind the procrastination.

You can see from the above examples that the next step can

be anything in the course of the day that causes inner and outer conflict. Be alert to such opportunities for growth. Very soon, you will realize that this daily mindfulness is a powerful tool toward transcendence and nonattachment, that is, the spiritual life.

There are minor next steps and major next steps. Minor ones are the stresses and conflicts that occur in the course of the day. They come and go, but they are valuable bricks and stones of growth if we attend to them.

Major next steps are those that are capable of creating turning points in life, such as the following:

- Recurring or protracted conflicts or difficulties in relationships

- Career conflicts, discomforts, or dilemmas

- Perceived character faults or weaknesses

- Recurring anxiety, worry, or major fears

- Yearning for inner or spiritual growth

Every person faces minor or major next steps all the time. Each of these next steps is a valuable opportunity for genuine growth. A clear self-transformative philosophy of life enables us to be alert to these opportunities and to take advantage of them. Thus will true growth be accelerated in our lives.

Self-Transformation and Youth

My colleagues and I have adapted the contents of the Self-Transformation Seminar into a four-day youth camp, called the Golden Link Youth Camp, in which young people from thirteen to twenty-five years of age learn its principles in an atmosphere of fun, activities, and teamwork. We have simplified the program but retained the essential elements, such as self-awareness processing, effective relationships, clarification of values, and feedbacking. Added to these are sessions that allow them to learn about acceptance of self and others, public speaking, and team-building. Many of them meet regularly after the camp. They organize community projects, sports festivals, service programs, learning sessions, and similar activities.

We had the opportunity of observing the effects of the Golden Link youth program on the lives of many young people. What we have seen in the past many years has surprised not only us facilitators, but also, more especially, the parents of these young people. The changes in the young people's behaviors, attitudes, relationships, values, and outlooks on life have convinced us that we are doing something right.

Larry was a poor college student whose mother was the sole breadwinner in the family. He had become a heavy alcoholic drinker, emptying an entire case of beer in one sitting. Many a time his mother would tearfully recount to close friends how Larry would sometimes come home and, finding that there was no food prepared yet, would throw frying pans around in the kitchen in anger.

One day, his mother learned about the Golden Link youth camps, and she persuaded her son to join. He did. The change in Larry's behavior was remarkable. He immediately quit drinking after the youth camp. His mother noted that not only was Larry no longer violent at home, but he regularly volunteered to do household work, such as fetching pails of water every morning from a community pump some distance away. (Their house didn't have tap water.) He was able to obtain a scholarship and finish his college education. He regularly volunteered to be a facilitator at youth camps. He was able to easily get a job and decided to pursue a degree in law. He is now a practicing lawyer and has come a long way from being a seemingly hopeless youth. His self-discipline is outstanding. His selflessness is genuine.

Jenn was a very timid girl who, when asked to speak to a group, would be so nervous that she would cry. She had very low self-esteem and didn't think that she could do significant things. During the youth camp, she said that she had a fear of earthworms and cried when she was confronted with these little creatures. She had become too self-effacing. When she overcame her fear of earthworms and public speaking during the youth camp, she realized the real possibilities of growth and improvement in her life. Jenn took this seriously and undertook an effort to improve herself. After several years, she has become a shining example of a young person who is self-confident, open, kind, cheerful, and effective in what she does. She now teaches, gives lectures, helps conduct youth camps, and serves as co-facilitator in the Self-Transformation Seminar.

Henry had become a curse to his father. He was the only son and had become so irresponsible and unreliable that his father had nothing but angry words for him whenever they saw each other. In turn, Henry showed not only disrespect, but also defiance toward his father. Despite his apparent intelligence, Henry had just flunked his third year in high school. He had become a heavy drinker and smoker and would sometimes come home at three o'clock a.m. after a drinking spree with his friends. His father could do nothing.

Then Henry joined the Golden Link Youth Camp held in the city where he lived. He was quite a problem on the first day. He would gather a group of participants and eat in a house outside the camping grounds in violation of the rules of the camp. He would regale the campers with sexual jokes that embarrassed the girls. But as the days passed, the contents of the camp began to touch him in a way that nobody expected.

Two weeks after the youth camp, I received a long-distance call from Henry, and he told me that he had good news. First, he had stopped smoking. Second, he had stopped drinking. His buddies had been wondering why he wasn't going with them anymore. But more important, he said that he now was on speaking terms with his father. His father had begun talking *with* him, rather than reprimanding him.

Two months later, Henry called again to tell me that he was now voluntarily helping in his father's business. Much later, he called again to tell me that he had passed the entrance test of one of the best universities in his region. In fact, he topped the exams.

I can cite innumerable cases like Larry, Jenn, and Henry whose growth directions drastically changed after they were exposed to the self-transformation process. Their experiences convinced me that the self-transformation process must be introduced to more and more young people through schools and youth groups.

Young people are more open to new ideas, attitudes, and behaviors, even if such ideas are seemingly in conflict with what society says. Their conditionings are not yet too deeply ingrained and hence are susceptible to contrary influences. The change in them at this age will have a significant effect on their adult lives. It will save them countless heartaches, sorrows, and fears. They will know how to deal with adversities, challenges, and temporary failures.

Self-transformation activities and lessons can be organized for young people, whether in or out of school environments. The learnings can supplement their home and school education. What is needed are more people who have gone through the self-transformation process to offer their time, energy, and insights to young people who need guidance in navigating this mystery called life and this concrete jungle called society. For information on how to present the self-transformation process to young people, you may contact us at the address found in appendix 3.

Self-Transformation and Education

It has always seemed strange to me that many essential skills and knowledge about life are not taught in schools. In school, children do not learn reliable information about happiness and unhappiness, about effective relationships, about handling emotions such as anger and depression, about self-mastery (not just mechanical discipline), about success in marital relationships, and about parenting. And yet they spend so much time learning about sines, cosines, polynomials, the products of this province or that region, the date when Magellan reached the Philippines and the names of his ships, the atomic weights of mercury and boron—tons of information that we are unlikely to use when we become adults.

Education must consist of at least two things: education for life and education to adapt to modern society. Modern education is primarily the second one, and the first one is often neglected.

Examples of the second kind of education are learning a language and learning the fundamentals of mathematics, history, social sciences, and similar subjects that are necessary for being effective in modern living. These also include courses that are short-lived. For example, becoming a computer programmer or legal management expert is linked to the social demands of the present generation. Centuries ago, it could have been military service or the priesthood. In the next century, it may be water engineering or something else. These are necessary, but they are, in the long run, secondary to the more basic needs of human growth and maturity.

We study courses that prepare us to earn enough money, but we don't study the art and science of happiness and fulfillment. We fall in love and marry hoping to live a happy life, but we don't learn how to have effective and loving relationships.

Education for life is essentially education for true human growth, irrespective of the culture that we are born into. This involves growth toward maturity with qualities such as those identified by Maslow for self-actualized people. I believe that education should incorporate this important aspect of learning. This aspect should be introduced not just at the collegiate level, but starting from nursery and elementary levels. The roots of character are formed in the early years; hence, what may be called transformative education should start early.

This kind of education requires three things: (1) a philosophy of life based on a more enlightened understanding of human nature and values; (2) a system of education that translates the philosophy into a program of teaching various subjects such as math, language, and history; and (3) a group of teachers whose lives embody the philosophy and who have been trained in implementing the system.

The Philosophy of Life

The philosophy of life that forms the foundation of transformative education is not a unitary philosophy that is fixed and dogmatic. It is a dynamic and creative one but is founded on the ageless wisdom, or perennial philosophy.

The ageless wisdom, or perennial philosophy, is hard to delineate and define, but it exists. It is not the invention of any single person, group, religion, culture, or tradition. It is a wisdom based on the accumulated experience of humanity. Its insights transcend cultural walls or sectarian narrowness. Its spirit is independent of any single group or movement in history. But the wisest traditions of each nation or culture are based on it. Its validity is recognized by intuition and common sense.

The ageless wisdom consists of an understanding of life and nature, that is, a comprehensive map of reality and a way of life based on such understanding. Its highest expressions are the mystical traditions of the various cultures such as mystical Christianity, mystical Buddhism, Kabbalah, Sufism, Vedanta, and Yoga. In human society, its principles are translated into modes of relationship and interaction that bring about ultimate harmony and unity. In personal life, it brings about inner peace, integration, and fulfillment.

The self-transformation process embodied in this book is rooted in the ageless wisdom. It brings together the insights of such representatives of the wisdom as Theosophy, Krishnamurti, Christian mysticism, transpersonal psychology, Zen, Ramana Maharshi, Yoga, Maslow, and a host of others.

Modern education is generally blind to the ageless wisdom. It is enthralled by the values of current society. The purpose of the average person is defined by the fleeting standards of what is currently popular: the Internet, stardom, politics, the best-seller list, and so on. Unfortunately, the meaning of human life has become defined by cultural icons.

Modern education is a docile instrument of social forces and thus serves the social structure, rather than the human being. In this sense, it fails in its important task of helping individuals attain their true potentials as human beings. Much of current education trains people to become efficient cogs in a huge social machine half-blindly invented by social evolution that measures life's meaning through such things as gross national income, foreign exchange reserves, rises in stock prices, box office hits, best-seller lists, increases in market share, front page recognition, or television coverage.

True education, although recognizing the need for people to adapt to the standards of current society, should at the same time teach students the wider view of life that transcends and encompasses economic survival and stability, social competition, and religious rivalry. It must help young people to

- understand love beyond the institution of marriage and the satisfaction of the senses.

- appreciate their humanity beyond nationality.

- see spirituality beyond religiosity.

- understand happiness beyond pleasure.

- see ethical rightness beyond cultural morality.

- pursue excellence rather than competition.

- see unity above insecurity.

The System of Education

Rooted in the ageless wisdom, education must devise a system, a program, or a scheme that enables young people to learn about living and, at the same time, adapt to current society. Such programs or policies should be based on core principles that are derived from the ageless wisdom.

Let's look at a few examples of how principles can be translated into the system.

Fear should not be used as a tool for motivating children to behave in a certain way. A source of human unhappiness and social conflict is the unwholesome conditioning of fear in individuals. It results in insecurity, aggressiveness, timidity, low self-esteem, unhappiness, and irrationality. Where do these fears come from? They are injected into the hearts of children by parents and teachers in order to impose discipline and condition the behavior of the children. It is important, therefore, that the system of education not utilize fear as an instrument of compulsion in education. It stunts growth, hinders true learning, obstructs creativity, and causes unhappiness.

A loving and caring environment generally produces an attitude and feeling in students that enhances growth, benevolence, cooperation, happiness, and well-being. Hence, the teachers and administrators must be capable of providing such an environment.

Children need to learn self-discipline or self-mastery. A loving atmosphere must not be interpreted as a license for children to do anything they want to do. Rules are necessary; this is obvious. Firmness must accompany love.

Let's look at how principles can be translated into the curriculum and teaching methods.

Learning must foster intelligence rather than mere accumulation of information. It is more important for students to understand why Columbus sought to travel westward than to memorize the date when he landed in the New World. It is more important for children to understand why the formula for a cylinder's volume is $v = \pi r^2 h$ than to pass exams by memorizing it. This is the development of intelligence, or the capacity to understand the underlying principles and their significance, so that they will be able to apply the learning to future circumstances.

Students must be motivated by excellence rather than competition. There should be no comparative grades or honors that pit one student against the others. Children who are slow in understanding mathematics are not necessarily less intelligent than their classmates. Human growth can't be adequately measured by single standards such as IQ tests or grades. It doesn't do justice to the multifaceted capabilities of a human being. That human capability cannot be simply measured by one standard is recognized by many schools of psychology today, such as Howard Gardner's theory of multiple intelligences (logical, linguistic, spatial, musical, kinesthetic, interpersonal, intrapersonal, naturalistic, and existential).

Example is one of the most powerful tools in education. The teachers must exemplify what they are teaching. If math teachers exhibit passion and interest for their subject matter, their example motivates the students to learn mathematics. When a teacher exudes enthusiasm in discussing history, such enthusiasm will infect the students. When the teacher doesn't use anger or shouting to resolve problematic situations, the students unconsciously adopt a similar way of meeting difficulties.

The Teachers

We come to a vital ingredient of an enlightened educational system: the presence of teachers who embody the philosophy and who are acquainted with the principles of such a system of education.

The teachers of transformative education are those who have grappled with the issues of life themselves. They are not perfect examples of the transformed individual, but they have struggled and learned the principles. They appreciate the purpose of enlightened education and sincerely try to live by its principles.

The teachers must possess the qualities of a self-transformed individual to a certain degree, specifically a loving nature, self-mastery, and a passionate interest in the subject they are teaching.

A loving attitude is not a skill. It is not a technique. It is a quality. A loving nature toward a student is like sunshine to a flower. It helps the flower bloom. Such a caring quality, coupled with self-mastery, exhibits patience in helping students learn. Teachers need to adjust to the pace of the student. They are glad to give extra time to students having difficulties. The teacher's passionate interest in the subject is the catalyst that awakens a corresponding enthusiasm in the student for the subject.

We need schools that offer transformative education. Such schools nurture young people who will be physically sound, emotionally wholesome, mentally alert, intelligent, responsible, sensitive to the common welfare, and prepared for the spiritual life. They are people who will not contribute to the mess of our present world. Their homes will not become additional trouble spots on earth. Rather, they are likely to contribute to the harmony and peace among people. They will be the living proofs that it is possible to be effective in human society without being insecure, antagonistic, competitive, acquisitive, and selfish, and that human happiness is possible amid the challenges and adversities of life.

Recommended Readings

One of the best ways to accelerate our understanding of life and reality is to read widely but selectively. In the past several thousand years, countless sages have grappled with the issues, the conflicts, and the mysteries of life and the cosmos, and they collectively can teach us important insights that we can't find in academic studies. Their teachings can help us, both in self-transformation and in seeing the larger and deeper view of reality. Some of them are listed here, with the caution that the list cannot hope to be exhaustive but is, rather, initiatory.

It is helpful to be familiar with certain popular self-help books, such as the works of Dale Carnegie, Napoleon Hill, and Anthony Robbins. They may have points of view that don't necessarily agree with this book, but in general, we can glean many practical insights from their writings. For example, much of Anthony Robbins's writings are about *reconditioning* ourselves, rather than transcending unwholesome conditioning through cleansing, release, or purification, which is the view adopted in the self-transformation process. This is a fundamental difference. Nonetheless, Robbins's and the other authors' books demonstrate that no individual need be at the mercy of their past. We can do something to change our lives.

From the popular self-help books, we turn our attention

to the perennial philosophy, or the ageless wisdom, of life. This wisdom doesn't teach skills or how to be successful in the world or how to be popular. Financial security is important, but it is only a small part of the larger picture of life. (In fact, overemphasis on financial security results in ineffectiveness in living.) The perennial philosophy goes beyond the cultural values of our time and gives us a wider and deeper perspective on life.

My own exposure to the ageless wisdom was through Theosophy. Although it is not the only one, it is, to my mind, one of the most comprehensive presentations of the wisdom. It also serves as a valuable background that helps us understand other books, philosophies, and religions. Below are three books to start with:

- *The Ancient Wisdom* by Annie Besant (Adyar: Theosophical Publishing House)

- *The Key to Theosophy* by H. P. Blavatsky (various editions, such as Pasadena: Theosophical University Press; Los Angeles: Theosophy Company; and Adyar: Theosophical Publishing House)

- *The Ocean of Theosophy* by William Q. Judge (various editions, such as Pasadena: Theosophical University Press and Los Angeles: Theosophy Company)

The ageless wisdom includes familiarity with various teachings of the inner side of nature that shed light on phenomena not well explained by science. This includes life after death, psychical phenomena, paranormal faculties, and the existence of *ch'i* or *prana*.

You may supplement these studies by reading the results of controlled researches in these fields, such as those of Kirlian photography, reincarnation research, Kilner screens, and the researches of the British and American Societies of Psychical Research. Examples of such work include:

- *20 Cases Suggestive of Reincarnation* by Dr. Ian Stevenson (Charlottesville: University Press of Virginia, 1974)

- *The Phoenix Fire Mystery* by J. Head and S. Cranston (New York: Julian Press, 1977); probably the best compilation of excerpts on reincarnation from various writers, scientists, philosophers, religious teachers, and scriptures

- *The Probability of the Impossible* by Dr. Thelma Moss (London: Routledge & Kegan Paul, 1976)

Modern statements of the ageless wisdom can be found in the writings of Ken Wilber, whose works and research encompass such a wide span of human knowledge that he has become perhaps the foremost modern writer on the perennial philosophy. A good introduction to his work is *The Essential Ken Wilber* (Boston: Shambhala, 2000). Wilber's works endeavor to integrate such diverse fields as psychology, sociology, modern physics, philosophy, comparative religion, and mysticism.

A special field of psychology that is worth being familiar with is transpersonal psychology. Here we suggest the works of Abraham Maslow and other psychologists, such as the following:

- *Motivation and Personality* by Abraham Maslow (New York: Harper and Row, 1987)

- *The Farther Reaches of Human Nature* by Abraham Maslow (New York: Arkana, 1993)

- *Religions, Values, and Peak-Experiences* by Abraham Maslow (Columbus: Ohio State University Press, 1964)

- *Psychosynthesis* by Roberto Assagioli (New York: Hobbs, Dorman, 1965)

- *Paths Beyond Ego* by Roger Walsh and Frances Vaughan (Eds.) (New York: Tarcher/Putnam, 1993)

One of the significant affirmations of the perennial philosophy is the spiritual unity of religions. Although religions today appear to be at loggerheads with each other, there is unanimity among perennial philosophers that, at the root level, all spiritual traditions are essentially in agreement. The following books are worth reading:

- *The Perennial Philosophy* by Aldous Huxley (London: Chatto & Windus, 1969)

- *The Transcendent Unity of Religions* by Fritjof Schuon (Wheaton, IL: Theosophical Publishing House, 1984)

- *The Mystery Teachings in World Religions* by Florice Tanner (Wheaton, IL: Theosophical Publishing House, 1973)

This brings us to the heart of religion: mysticism, or mystical experience. Self-transformation eventually leads to the mystical life. As one writer put it, "There is no other way to go." Hence, familiarity with mystical consciousness is an essential part of our readings. There are many excellent books on this subject. I suggest a few:

- "Mysticism," by William James (one of the last chapters of his book *Varieties of Religious Experience*, New York: Triumph Books, 1991)

- *Mysticism* by Evelyn Underhill (Mineola, NY: Dover, 2002)

- *Understanding Mysticism* by Richard Woods (Ed.) (Garden City, NY: Image Books, 1980)

An appreciation of the different time-tested paths toward spirituality is important, such as the following:

- *Yoga Sutras of Patanjali.* This is the essential sourcebook on Yoga, written about 2,500 years ago. There are many translations of this work with commentaries. I. K. Taimni's *The Science of Yoga* (Adyar: Theosophical Publishing House) is one of the most comprehensive.

- *The Inner Life* by Hazrat Inayat Khan (Boston: Shambhala, 1997). This is a book on mysticism by a Sufi.

- *The Essentials of Zen Buddhism* by D. T. Suzuki (Westport, CT: Greenwood Press, 1973). It is very helpful to be familiar with the mysticism of Buddhism, such as Zen, *vipassana* meditation, and Tibetan Buddhism.

- *The Interior Castle* by Teresa of Avila (New York: Paulist Press, 1979) is a description of the layers of consciousness that lead to union.

- *The Spiritual Teaching of Ramana Maharshi* (Boston: Shambhala, 1972). Sri Ramana is considered to be one of the true sages of the twentieth century. His teachings are simple and use the "self-inquiry" or *vichara* approach to meditation.

The works of J. Krishnamurti are particularly recommended to the student of self-transformation. His teachings present one of the clearest and most direct approaches to awareness and the transcendent life. They don't contain jargon or technicalities that tend to obfuscate rather than clarify. Read any compilation of his talks, particularly the following:

- *The First and Last Freedom* (New York: Harper & Row, 1975). This is a collection of the various themes of his talks.

- *Life Ahead* (Ojai, CA: Krishnamurti Publications, 2000). This is a book for young people. It contains a clear discussion about the many conditionings that people acquire as they grow up.

- *Commentaries on Living, Series 1, 2, and 3.* (Wheaton: Theosophical Publishing House, 1956)

The practice of meditation is an important part of the self-transformation process. It is therefore helpful to be familiar with the principles and the steps in proper meditation. In addition to the books mentioned above such as the *Yoga Sutras* of Patanjali, a few more books are suggested:

- *How to Meditate* by Lawrence LeShan (Boston: Little, Brown, 1999)

- *Journey of Awakening* by Ram Dass (New York: Bantam, 1990)

- *Concentration and Meditation* by Christmas Humphreys (Baltimore: Penguin, 1970)

One of the crucial segments of the self-transformation process is self-awareness processing, which involves the purification of the psyche of unresolved psychological issues and memories. An understanding of the principles involving *ch'i* and its movements is helpful in this regard. The best sources are books on acupuncture that identify the fourteen main meridians of the body.

Finally, it is helpful to learn about effective relationships from the insights of many authors. In addition to the works of Dale Carnegie, I recommend *People Skills* by John Bolton (New York: Simon & Schuster, 1986).

From the above list of recommended readings, you can branch out into deeper specialized studies.

Self-Inventory

The following self-inventory should help you clarify your growth directions in life. The descriptions are only suggestive and are not meant to be completely accurate for everyone. The number "1" indicates that you have attained full mastery over that particular aspect, and a "5" indicates that you are almost overwhelmed or overcome by a lack of mastery of that aspect. Rewrite the descriptions to make them more suitable to your situation. Each one of these aspects is within your power to control. Decide which area you need to improve upon.

ASPECT	1	2	3	4	5
Irritation	Not an issue	Seldom	Occasionally	Often	Very often
Anger	Not an issue	Very seldom, and only slightly	Occasionally	Often and with intensity	Very often, with tendency toward violence
Resentment	Resents no one; tries to send sincerely helpful thoughts to those hostile to oneself	Dislikes some people, but can relate to them harmoniously	Resents a few people; avoids them	Harbors anger and strong resentment of certain people; wishes them ill	Has strong hatred toward certain people; wants to retaliate
Fear	Has no fear	Has negligible reactions to threatening situations	Fears certain things and avoids them	Has strong fears	Has phobia(s) affecting one's life, happiness, or career
Tension/Stress	Is aware of slight tension; can relax easily and quickly	Feels tension but is able to relax afterward	Notices tiredness or stress	Gets tired easily; has pains	Is highly stressed, high strung, and easily angered
Worry	Handles problems immediately and knows how to prevent worry; accepts unavoidable situations	Is occasionally bothered by unresolved worries	Has worries and feels the burden	Worries a lot, affecting one's mind and health	Is a chronic worrier; finds it hard to sleep; needs medicine or tranquilizers

ASPECT	1	2	3	4	5
Family Relationships	Harmonious, caring, and meaningful	Generally harmonious; minor communication problems	Occasional friction, anger, and resentment	Often conflicted; avoids other family members; does not enjoy being at home	Almost intolerable; relationships on the verge of breaking up
Work Relationships	Harmonious, caring, and meaningful	Generally harmonious; minor communication problems	Occasional friction, anger, and resentment	Often conflicted; avoids other workers; does not enjoy being at work	Almost intolerable; on the verge of leaving or changing work
Social Relationships	Harmonious, caring, and meaningful	Generally harmonious; minor communication problems	Occasional friction, anger, and resentment	Often conflicted; avoids others and does not enjoy their company	Almost nonexistent; rarely engages with others
Work and Career	Fulfilling, highly motivating, and productive	Satisfactory	Tolerable; sometimes fulfilling; at times unhappy	Unsatisfactory	Causes feelings of resentment, unproductivity, unhappiness
Attachment to Things	Values and takes care of possessions, but fully accepts their loss if necessary	Has concern about loss of job, possessions, or reputation, but handles adversities well	Feels apprehensive about losing job, possessions, reputation, etc.	Feels strongly apprehensive about losing job, possessions, reputation, etc.	Constantly fears losing possessions, finances, status, reputation, etc.

ASPECT	1	2	3	4	5
Attachment to People	Caring and loving, but can fully accept parting or loss if necessary	Concerned about loss or departure of loved one, but can handle it	Apprehensive about loss of loved one	Bothered by recurring thought of loss of loved one	Constantly afraid of losing loved one; daily effectiveness affected
Inner Peace	Generally serene; able to face and handle adversities with calmness	Generally contented	Contented, but often complains about things	Unhappy with one's lot in life	Often feels depressed, unhappy, or lonely; angry with life
Self-Centeredness	Does not mind personal inconveniences; cheerfully gives way to others on personal issues; spontaneously helpful without thought of recognition	Helpful; easily gets over the thoughtlessness of others without suppression	Tries to be fair, but is hurt or offended when personal needs or wants are not met; occasionally helpful but does not go out of the way to serve	Insists on one's personal needs and wants; feels bad if not met; not motivated to help or be of service to others	Angers easily at personal inconveniences; easily hurt and offended; strongly driven to gain advantage over others, even if unethical

Becoming a Facilitator

Many people who have attended the Self-Transformation Seminar ask how they can become facilitators of the seminar. The first prerequisite is to have attended the seminar. It is conducted in various countries, such as in the United States, Australia, New Zealand, India, and the Philippines, by individuals or groups that have been trained as facilitators.

The person interested in becoming a facilitator must possess certain minimum qualities such as patience, communication skills, and genuine interest in helping people to resolve basic problems in living. The training of a facilitator takes years, and the trainee must be ready to sustain the effort to deepen his or her capacity to help in the transformation process of other people.

The Self-Transformation Seminar is not simply about learning skills, although it involves the learning of many skills that are useful throughout life. It is about a way of living, founded on a life view rooted in the ageless wisdom. It is an understanding of who we are as human beings; it is about clarifying what is important and what is less important, about self-mastery, about relationships, and about the transcendence of the chronic conflicts that characterize daily life. Thus, in its deeper aspects, the seminar is a preparation for the higher life, the mystical life.

Helping the transformation effort of other people is a noble task. It is also a deep responsibility. It requires facilitators to not only undertake the difficult quest of understanding life and themselves, but also develop qualities that will prepare them to effectively assist other people in their own transformation processes.

Life is immensely complex. In understanding it more fully, we can't limit ourselves to our respective areas of specialization, like a doctor who is good at curing diseases but fails miserably in dealing with marital or family problems. Genuine self-transformation involves a well-balanced and well-rounded wisdom regarding key aspects of living. As facilitators, then, we need to widen our scope of comprehension such that we understand the dynamics of those key aspects—values, sorrows, pains, desires, fears, life's purpose, relationships, the nature of consciousness, and so on. In deepening such understanding, our studies necessarily bring us to the fields of science, mysticism, psychology, religious experience, philosophy, physiology, social sciences, and communication arts.

Although we can't become experts in such a broad spectrum of human knowledge, we can at least comprehend well those aspects that are relevant to the realization of our higher potential. For this reason, the nurturing of a facilitator necessarily takes years. It requires cognitive understanding of the nature of life and its processes; an intensive exploration of effective approaches to the resolution of conflicts in our own lives that eventually prepare us for the transcendent or spiritual life; and the development of skills in counseling and communication—public speaking, group dynamics, and organizing—and the special capacity to help others in self-awareness processing.

If you are interested in attending the seminar or training as a facilitator, please contact:

The Philippine Theosophical Institute
1 Iba Street, Quezon City
Philippines
Email: philtheos@gmail.com; v.haochin@gmail.com
Website: www.selftransformation.net

Notes

Chapter 2

1. I refer to self-transformation as a process in the general sense of an "action of moving forward progressively from one point to another on the way to completion." This should not be confused with the special use of the terms *process* and *processing* in subsequent chapters of this book, specifically, the *self-awareness processing*. The latter is but a part of the entire self-transformation process.

Chapter 3

1. W. Kilner, *The Aura* (New York: Samuel Weiser, 1973).
2. Thelma Moss, *The Probability of the Impossible* (New York: New American Library, 1974), 23 ff.
3. Paramahansa Yogananda, *Autobiography of a Yogi* (Los Angeles: Self-Realization Fellowship, 1974), 368 ff., 461–72.

Chapter 5

1. C. G. Jung, *Selected Writings* (London: Fontana Paperbacks, 1983).
2. Roberto Assagioli, *Psychosynthesis* (New York: Viking Press, 1971).
3. Abraham Maslow, *Motivation and Personality* (New York: Harper and Row, 1970), 153–174.
4. Gordon W. Allport, *Personality and Social Encounter* (Boston: Beacon Press, 1964), 162.
5. Alan W. Watts, *Psychotherapy East and West* (New York: New American Library, 1963), 18.
6. Psalms 110:4; Hebrews 5:4–6, 6:20, 7:1–3, 20–23.

7. Hebrews 12:23; Ephesians 4:13; 1 Corinthians 2:6–8; Matthew 5:48.

8. Karl Rahner, et al., *Sacramentum Mundi: An Encyclopedia of Theology*, vol. 3 (New York: Herder and Herder, 1970), 401.

9. Adapted from C. W. Leadbeater, *Man, Visible and Invisible* (Chennai: Theosophical Publishing House, 1925), plate 4.

Chapter 7

1. William James, *Varieties of Religious Experience* (Grand Rapids, MI: Christian Classics Ethereal Library), 236.

Chapter 11

1. Experiments conducted in which adrenaline was injected into subjects to imitate the effects of the sympathetic nervous system show that the subjects did not feel emotions. See S. Schachter and J. E. Singer, "Cognitive, social, and physiological determinants of emotional state," *Psychological Review* 69 (1962), 379–399; cited in David G. Myers, *Psychology*, 4th ed. (New York: Worth Publishers, 1995), 456.

2. Different psychologists have different lists of basic emotions. There can be as few as two (happiness and sadness) and as many as eleven (anger, aversion, courage, dejection, desire, despair, fear, hate, hope, love, and sadness). The list varies according to the criteria chosen by the psychologist. For various lists, see A. Ortony and T. J. Turner, "What's basic about basic emotions?", *Psychological Review* 97 (1990), 315–331.

3. E. B. Ebbesen, B. Duncan, and V. J. Konecni, "Effects of content of verbal aggression on future verbal aggression: A field experiment," *Journal of Experimental Social Psychology* 11 (1975), 192–204; cited in David G. Myers, *Psychology*, 4th ed. (New York: Worth Publishers, 1995), 446.

Chapter 18

1. Victor Parachin, *365 Good Reasons to Be a Vegetarian* (New York: Avery Publishing, 1998), 10, 62.

2. T. Colin Campbell and Thomas M. Campbell II, *The China Study* (Dallas: BenBella Books, 2006), 7.

3. Parachin, *365 Good Reasons*, 95.

Chapter 22

1. Swami Prabhavananda, *The Sermon on the Mount According to Vedanta* (New York: New American Library, 1963), 65.
2. Ibid.
3. Mabel Collins, *Light on the Path* (Chennai: Theosophical Publishing House, 1911), 19.

Chapter 23

1. *Encyclopaedia Britannica*, Mysticism, Britannica CD 2000 Deluxe Edition.
2. Evelyn Underhill, *Mysticism* (New York: E. P. Dutton, 1961), 72.
3. *Encyclopaedia Britannica*, Mysticism.
4. Geoffrey Hodson, *Call to the Heights* (Wheaton, IL: Theosophical Publishing House, 1975).
5. *Encyclopaedia Britannica*, Maqam, Britannica CD 2000 Deluxe Edition.
6. Richard Bucke, *Cosmic Consciousness* (New York: E. P. Dutton, 1969).
7. *Encyclopaedia Britannica*, Hal, Britannica CD 2000 Deluxe Edition.
8. *Encyclopaedia Britannica*, Sufism.

Chapter 24

1. Evelyn Underhill, *Practical Mysticism* (New York: E. P. Dutton, 1915), 37.
2. Sigmund Freud, *Collected Papers*, vol. 2, quoted in Maslow, *Motivation and Personality*, 207 (see chap. 5, n. 3).
3. J. Krishnamurti, *Collected Works*, vol. 17 (Dubuque, IA: Kendall/Hunt, 1992), 35.
4. Ibid., 208
5. Maslow, *Motivation and Personality*, 207 (see chap. 5, n. 3).
6. Ibid., 210.

Chapter 25

1. I. K. Taimni, *The Science of Yoga* (Chennai: Theosophical Publishing House, 1961).
2. H. P. Blavatsky, *The Key to Theosophy*, Glossary.

Chapter 26

1. Thomas Merton, *Zen and the Birds of Appetite* (New York: New Directions, 1968).

2. Elaine MacInnes, *Teaching Zen to Christians* (Manila: Theosophical Publishing House, 1993).

3. Hazrat Inayat Khan, *The Inner Life* (Boston: Shambhala, 1997), 60.

4. Abraham H. Maslow, *Religions, Values, and Peak-Experiences* (London: Penguin, 1976), 20.

Glossary

aggressiveness. An approach to handling interpersonal conflict characterized by accusatory and judgmental words, often accompanied with hostile tone and emotions. It is an approach that tends to prolong or worsen the conflict. See also *assertiveness*; *timid*.

assertiveness. An approach to handling interpersonal conflict characterized by the ability to express one's feelings or views without offending the other person. It tends to use statements that start with "I" rather than "You" and expresses feelings without accusing or judging. See also *aggressiveness*; *timid*.

awareness. A term that has a spectrum of meanings, from awareness of something to pure awareness without any specific objects. In the self-transformation process, self-awareness refers to awareness of the sensations, perceptions, and phenomena occurring in one's body, emotions, and mind. In meditation, awareness starts from awareness of something to awareness without any object. See also *meditation*.

basic emotions. Emotions that are not derived from other kinds of emotion. Among negative emotions, the following are considered basic emotions: fear, anger, hurt, aversion, dejection, and guilt. All other negative emotions such as anxiety, worry, jealousy, depression, etc., are derivatives of these basic emotions or are combinations of several basic emotions. Thus resentment is a hurt mixed with irritation or anger.

ch'i. See *energy*.

conditioning. An automatic reaction to a given stimulus (perception, imagination, memory, etc.), or a fixed, acquired habit or behavior. Conditionings include fear reactions, prejudices, likes, dislikes, attitudes, etc. When unexamined, these conditionings largely determine the way of life of the individual.

congestion. The accumulation of an energy in a specific part of the body, such as the chest or the head, resulting in sensations of discomfort, tightness, heaviness, or pain. This is due to holding back or freezing the energy in that location rather than allowing it to flow naturally. The congestion is released and a normal state is attained through the self-awareness processing. See also *emotional processing*; *energy*.

cultural values. Values adopted or promoted by society, which tend to condition the world view of individuals as they grow up. Cultural values include some religious values. They may change over time and can include many superstitious and irrational beliefs. See also *universal values*; *personal values*.

emotional processing. The awareness of the discomfort in the body while undergoing emotional distress (fear, anger, hurt, depression, etc.), and, with the help of deep breathing, letting the energy congestions in the body flow and be released, leading to a state of relaxation and the disappearance of the distressful emotional reaction. See also *scanning; self-awareness processing*.

energy. Unless defined otherwise, *energy* refers to the semi-physical energy that circulates throughout the body through the meridians of acupuncture. It has been called *ch'i* (or *qi* in pinyin), *prana*, bioplasmic energy, orgone, odic force, animal magnetism, etc. It is what is activated when a person feels an emotion. It in turn stimulates physiological or biochemical changes in the body. This energy is to be distinguished from the energy of the psyche or consciousness, which is more subtle. See also *congestion*.

expectations. What one expects others to do, which can result in frustration or emotional pain when unfulfilled. There are two kinds of expectations: personal expectations and relationship expectations. Personal expectations are those motivated by personal needs and desires, and can lead to unhappiness when unfulfilled. Relationship expectations are those created by agreed relationships (whether implied or explicit) such as marriage, employment, friendship, etc. Relationship expectations need not cause personal frustration and unhappiness if not met.

expression of emotions. Expressing feelings such as shouting, hitting a pillow, crying, etc. It is distinguished from the release of the energy connected with the emotions. Expression does not necessarily release the energy, and release need not entail expression. Thus a person who hits a pillow in anger may still be angry afterward, while a person who releases the energy connected with anger will cease to be angry or resentful of the person. See also *release of feeling-energy*.

field of attention. The field of awareness when one is conscious of something. It is to be distinguished from the peripheral consciousness, which is next to it. See also *peripheral consciousness*.

functional zero level of tension. A state of the body where no unnecessary tension is exerted on the muscles other than those involved in a specific activity being done at the moment, such as reading a book, walking, or playing tennis.

higher triangle. The individuality consisting of the higher mind, the transcendent consciousness, and the True Self. See also *lower triangle*; *personality*; *individuality*.

individuality. The inner self consisting of the higher mind, the spiritual consciousness, and the Self, or spirit within. It is contrasted to the personality, composed of the lower mind, the emotions, and the body, including the subconscious mind. The individuality is symbolized by the upright triangle. See also *personality*.

integration. The harmonious functioning of the individuality (or inner self) and personality (or outer self), with the former controlling and determining the behavior of the latter.

love. A selfless concern for the welfare of another or of others, as distinguished from a self-centered concern that is often mistaken for love, such as missing a person, feeling jealous, etc. Love is essentially unconditional and does not change, even if the other person changes. In its expression it can be firm and assertive, and will act according to the best welfare of all concerned, rather than try to please for fear of losing the affection of the other. See also *expectations*.

lower triangle. The personality consisting of the body, emotions, and lower mind. See also *higher triangle*; *personality*; *individuality*.

map of reality. One's personal understanding of oneself, of life, of nature, and of the cosmos. Such a map may contain erroneous parts, which then misleads the person into living according to such mistaken views. To the extent that maps are defective, lives may become less effective, resulting in frustration, pain, sorrow, disharmony, etc.

meditation. A state of awareness undisturbed by the uncontrolled movement of thoughts, emotions, and perceptions. True meditation is the age-old gateway to the awakening of spiritual or mystical consciousness. It is different from certain popular practices (also called meditation) that involve the relaxation of the body, the settling down of the psyche, or the attainment of a brain state conducive to the pro duction of alpha brain waves. These are useful, but do not constitute the essence of spiritual meditation. Some of the well-known approaches to spiritual meditation are Yoga, Zen, *vipassana* or mindfulness, and awareness. All of them involve preparations that nurture self-discipline in the body, pranic body, emotions, and thoughts. See also *transcendence*; *mystical consciousness*; *spiritual*.

meridians. The channels through which the *ch'i* energy flows. There are fourteen major meridians in acupuncture practice, and many other minor ones. The meridians have points along the channels where energy congestions can occur.

mystical consciousness. Awareness of a level of consciousness beyond thoughts, images, and intentions. It is synonymous with spiritual or contemplative consciousness.

next step. An opportunity for growth that one faces at any given moment. When one feels distressed about an incident, this distress is a symptom that something is not yet mastered or learned. A person can look into oneself or the situation to see what can be learned; this is the next step of growth.

peripheral consciousness. The field of consciousness next to the normal field of attention or awareness. One tends to be oblivious to the content of this peripheral field of consciousness, not because it is subliminal or subconscious, but because one's attention is exclusively focused on something else. A person can become aware of the contents by a diffusion of one's field of attention, thus encompassing a larger part of its periphery. The peripheral consciousness is distinguished from the preconscious mind in that the former refers to the perception of present contents of the mind, such as a feeling, a tension, an attitude, while the preconscious mind can contain anything that may not be presently relevant, such as memories of what was done yesterday. See also *preconscious mind*; *field of attention*; *subconscious mind*.

personality. The outer self of a human being, composed of the body, emotions, and lower mind. The personality is subject to conditioning and is driven by needs and desires, thus tending to be self-centered. See also *individuality*.

personal values. The hierarchy of values that are determined by one's personal preferences, such as interests, career, tastes, hobbies, likes, dislikes, etc. See also *cultural values; universal values*.

prana. See *energy*.

preconscious mind. A part of the mind that is readily accessible to one's conscious mind but which, in the moment, is not in the field of one's attention. See also *peripheral consciousness; subconscious mind; field of attention*.

processing. See *self-awareness processing*.

psyche. The emotional and mental nature of a person. The psyche belongs to the personality.

push button. A subconscious conditioning that produces a fixed reaction pattern when stimulated or provoked. It is generally acquired through experience and can evoke pleasurable reactions, such as excitement, or painful ones, such as fear. See also *conditioning*.

reaction. An automatic conditioned action triggered by a stimulus or perception. A reaction arises out of one's conditioning, and hence may be performed without thought, deliberation, or wisdom. A reaction may even be irrational, such as fear when seeing the picture of a snake. In contrast to this, a response is an action arising from one's inner self; hence, it has been weighed in relation to one's deeper values and is free from the conditioned reaction of the personality, or lower triangle. See also *response*.

release of feeling-energy. Allowing the energy connected with an emotion to flow naturally using self-awareness processing or a similar approach. The release effectively resolves the associated emotion such as fear or anger. It is to be distinguished from expression of emotions, such as hitting a pillow in anger, which does not necessarily resolve the anger. See also *expression of emotions*.

response. An action or answer to a stimulus, perception, or situation. A response, as used in this book, comes from the higher triangle—either from the higher mind only or with intuition—in contrast to a reaction, which comes from the personality's conditionings, and hence tends to be more superficial. See also *reaction*.

scanning. The awareness of any tension or discomfort in the physical body while doing deep abdominal breathing, and the normalization of such tension. See also *emotional processing*.

self; Self. The word *self* generally refers to the personality or outer self. When it is capitalized, it refers to the inner self, at the core of which is the spirit or *atma*.

self-awareness. In the self-transformation process, this refers to awareness of the various facets of the self-personality: body, feelings, and thoughts. It must be distinguished from pure awareness, which has no object for its perception.

self-awareness processing. Being aware of a physiological reaction or sensation while doing deep abdominal breathing without attempting to change, suppress, or fight such reaction or sensation. See also *emotional processing*; *scanning*.

self-mastery. Mastery by the inner self, or individuality, over the habits and behaviors of the personality, or outer self.

self-transformation. A process characterized by two major aspects: (1) the awakening or strengthening of one's individuality or inner nature, and (2) the transformation of the outer self or personality to become congruent with the individuality.

seven-day program. A resolution to do a task or to practice a behavior regularly for seven consecutive days as a way of training the personality to be obedient to one's higher will. The resolution should be specific and measurable, and should entail some degree of difficulty. A method for accomplishing it should be specified.

spiritual. A level of consciousness that transcends the mind. It has been called mystical, contemplative, transcendental, *buddhi*, etc. It is a state of being rather than a belief system. It thus transcends the theologies or dogmas of religions. See also *mysticism*; *transcendence*.

subconscious mind. The layer of consciousness that is normally hidden from one's consciousness, but the contents of which can surface to the conscious mind. While this term is often interchanged with *unconscious*, it is helpful to distinguish the two. The contents of the subconscious mind have functional interactive relationships with the conscious mind, while those of the unconscious mind are those that do not, and may never, surface to the conscious mind. See also *preconscious mind*; *field of attention*.

subjective unit of distress (SUD). A simple method of determining the level of distress a person is experiencing at any moment. It is generally asked in the following way: "On a scale of 0 to 10, where zero means you are completely relaxed and comfortable and 10 means you are intolerably tense or distressed, what number level do you feel right now?"

timid. Being afraid to express oneself or one's feelings, especially in a conflict situation where one is bothered, hurt, angry, etc. The person tends to suppress the unresolved feelings. It is an ineffective mode of dealing with conflict. See also *aggressiveness*; *assertiveness*.

transcendence. Going beyond the levels of experience of the body, feelings, and mind; reaching or awakening a level of consciousness that is beyond the limitations of the personality and its conditionings. It is the realm of the mystical, the spiritual, or the contemplative. It involves the emergence of transpersonal consciousness, such as *buddhi*, *prajna*, or true intuition. See also *mysticism*; *spiritual*.

universal values. Values that are shared by all human beings regardless of culture or epoch. Examples of these are truth, sincerity, justice, beauty, harmony, etc. Values are universal either from the inherent nature of the value (such as truth, which is by its nature preferred over illusion), or from the make-up of human nature (such as humanity's natural pursuit for happiness). It is distinguished from cultural values, which change according to age and place, and from personal values, which vary from person to person. Conflicts and disharmony arise when personal and cultural values are not in alignment with universal values. Universal values are non-negotiable, so to speak. They do not adjust to suit a culture or a person. See also *cultural values*; *personal values*.

Index

Boldface indicates glossary entry   f indicates figure

A

abdominal breathing, 52–53, 63–65, 64f
abstract thought, 26–27, 247
acceptance of self, 41
achievement, 207–8
active listening, 150–55, 152f
acupuncture meridians, 51–52, 63, 83–85, 84f, **316**
aerobics, 186–87
affirmation, 168
ageless wisdom, 285, 292–93
aggressiveness, 156–61, 157f, **311**
ahwal (spiritual states), 230
alcohol, 187
Al-insan al kamil (Al-Jili), 43–44
Al-Jili, 43–44
Allport, Gordon, 40, 42
alpha state, 239
Ancient Wisdom, The (Besant), 31, 292
anger
    degrees of, 300

derivatives of, 105–6
development of, 104–6, 110f, 111
felt in head, 83, 109
animal magnetism, 25
animals, 185
anxiety, 102–3
Apollonius of Tyana, 40
appreciation, 42, 171
arhats, 43, 231
Aristotle, 132
Arjuna, 220
arupa manas (higher mental), 25f, 26–27
asanas (postures), 242, 243f, 244
Assagioli, Roberto, 40, 45
assertiveness, **311**
    harmonious, 150, 156–61, 157f
    in love, 169–70
associations, 233
astral body, 31–32
atma (spirit), 25f, 27, 44f, 46, 227, 243f

D

F

G

J

K

M

T

Quest Books
encourages open-minded inquiry into
world religions, philosophy, science, and the arts
in order to understand the wisdom of the ages,
respect the unity of all life, and help people explore
individual spiritual self-transformation.

Its publications are generously supported by
The Kern Foundation,
a trust committed to Theosophical education.

Quest Books is the imprint of
the Theosophical Publishing House,
a division of the Theosophical Society in America.
For information about programs, literature,
on-line study, membership benefits, and international centers,
see www.theosophical.org
or call 800-669-1571 or (outside the U.S.) 630-668-1571.

Related Quest Titles
Finding Deep Joy, by Robert Ellwood
Finding the Quiet Mind, by Robert Ellwood
The Meditative Path, by John Cianciosi
*The One True Adventure: Theosophy
and the Quest for Meaning*, by Joy Mills

To order books or a complete Quest catalog,
call 800-669-9425 or (outside the U.S.) 630-665-0130.